STRATEGIC CAREER ENGAGEMENT

The DEFINITIVE GUIDE for GETTING HIRED and PROMOTED

DONN LeVIE JR.

KINGS CROWN PUBLISHING

STRATEGIC CAREER ENGAGEMENT:
THE DEFINITIVE GUIDE FOR GETTING HIRED AND PROMOTED

Library of Congress Cataloging-in-Publication Data

LeVie Jr., Donn 1951 –

Other books by Donn LeVie Jr.:

- Confessions of a Hiring Manager Rev 2.0: Getting to and Staying at the Top of the Hiring Manager's Short List in a Confused Economy (Second Edition) (2012)

- It's All About HYMN: Essays on Reclaiming Sacred and Traditional Music for Worship (2008)

- Instrumental Influences: Reflections on the Classical Guitar from the Instrument's Most Influential Performers and Pedagogues (2011)

ISBN-13: 978-1-937678-08-1
ISBN-10: 1-937678-08-3

Volume discounts of Donn's books are available for corporations, associations, universities and colleges, business and trade schools, and military organizations. Contact the publisher for more information.

Contents

INTRODUCTION _____ 1

ONE: The Hiring Manager's Side of the Desk _____ 5

TWO: The Hiring Manager's Dilemma _____ 9

Who and What Is a "Hiring Manager"? _____ 11

Hiring the Wrong Employee: Why It Happens _____ 13

Hiring the Right Employee: Why It Happens _____ 14

Why Hiring Managers Are Often Hesitant Participants in the Hiring Process __ 14

Hiring Managers' Prejudices and Presuppositions _____ 15

Positive Prejudice _____ 16

The Bully Mindset _____ 17

Excluding the Tails _____ 18

*Objective Assessment Tools: How Valid and Useful Are They for Hiring
Decisions?* _____ 19

Job Bots: One Possible Reason You Didn't Get the Job _____ 21

What's in a Name? _____ 26

What About the Ethnicity of the Hiring Manager? _____ 28

The Question of Overqualification _____ 29

Referral Hires, Non-Referral Hires, and Internal Hires _____ 30

Recruitment Marketing Effectiveness _____ 32

Social Network Sites as an Exclusionary Recruiting Tool _____ 35

THREE: Raise Your Likeability Factor _____ 39

Challenges and Issues in the Hiring Manager's Domain _____ 42

Job Interview Context: Social and Situational Influences on Hiring Decisions 47

Finding the Right Balance of Impression Management _____ 49

The Language of Impression Management _____ 51

*The Likeability Factor and Impression Management Are Forms of Persuasion
You Should Master* _____ 52

FOUR: What Hiring Managers are Looking for in Candidates _____ 55

What Is "Talent" in the Job Market? _____ 56

The Knowing-Doing Gap in Talent Management _____ 58

Guarding Against Groupthink _____ 60

Creating Valueocity _____ 60

Where Candidates Fail _____ 61

Creating Functional Expertise from Tasks and Duties _____ 61

Hiring Manager and Candidate Common Ground _____ 63

FIVE: The Candidate Strategy _____ **65**

Create a Professional Brand and Generate Positive Associations _____ 65

The Importance of Creating a Personal Connection _____ 66

True Story: Branding Gone Wrong + Groupthink + Poor Relationship
    Management = Major Fail _____ 69

Getting into Their Heads: Associative Models _____ 70

Promoting Your Professional Brand in the Marketplace ____ 73

Protecting Your Professional Brand _____ 74

Watch Your *&^%@# Language! _____ 75

Moving Beyond the Professional Brand: Building Your Platform _____ 76

The New Way to Network _____ 78

What Is Your Value Proposition? _____ 81

Be Aware of Your Blind Spots _____ 83

Understand the Factors That Influence Your Promotability _____ 84

SIX: The Role of Professional Credentials in the Job Market _____ **89**

Core Competencies _____ 89

When Credentials Attack _____ 92

SEVEN: Selling the Future Benefits of Your Expertise in Cover Letters _ **95**

Use Direct Mail Strategies to Create an Effective Cover Letter _____ 96

Drilling Deeper into the Cover Letter Strategy _____ 99

Other Cover Letter Information Blocks _____ 104

Converting Features of Past Experience to Future Benefits of Expertise in a
    Cover Letter _____ 105

EIGHT: Advanced Résumé Therapy _____ **107**

Use the Correct Résumé Format for Your Purpose _____ 108

The Reverse Chronological Format: Looking for a Job in the Same Field ___ 109

The Functional Format: Entering/Re-Entering the Workforce or Changing Careers _____ *109*

The Curriculum Vitae (CV): Moving into Academia or Health Care _____ *110*

Understand the Difference Between Task Completion and Accomplishment _____ *110*

For the Last Time: No Objective Statements, Please! _____ *112*

Words Can Hurt You _____ *114*

Tips for Creating an Achievement-Focused Résumé _____ *117*

Keep a Log of Project Success for Future Use _____ *118*

Assign Quantitative Value to Your Accomplishments _____ *119*

Converting Tasks and Duties to Functional Expertise _____ *121*

Word of Caution: Beware of Résumé Fraud _____ *123*

NINE: Fine-Tuning Your Job Interview Strategy _____ **129**

Proven Question for NOT Getting the Job _____ *130*

The Worst Response to an Inevitable Interview Question _____ *131*

Situational Interview Approaches _____ *132*

Going Outside the Box for a Solution to a Problem _____ *133*

Reframe Your Perceptions of Confidence to Overcome the Impostor Syndrome _____ *135*

How Nonverbal Behaviors Influence Interviewers _____ *137*

How to Work Job Interviews at Job or Career Fairs _____ *138*

TEN: The Post-Interview Strategy _____ **143**

The Continuous Promotion Approach _____ *145*

ELEVEN: After Saying "Yes" to the Job Offer _____ **151**

Don't Be a Cubicle Crawler _____ *153*

Why the Organization May Not Embrace Your Ideas for Change ____ *156*

TWELVE: Making the Jump: Career Transitions _____ **159**

From Public Sector to Private Sector _____ *159*

Let's Get Practical _____ *160*

The Public Sector Résumé _____ *160*

Moving to the Private Sector _____ *162*

THIRTEEN: They Can't Pay You Enough to be Miserable: Time to Move On _____ 165

FOURTEEN: Becoming an Authority _____ 171

Postscript _____ 177

About the Author_____ 181

Appendix A: Bring Donn LeVie Jr. to Your Organization _____ 183

What Others Are Saying About Donn LeVie Jr. Seminars, Presentations, and Career Consultations _____ 184

Appendix B: Other Career Strategy Books by Donn LeVie Jr._____ 187

More Valuable Career Strategy Resources _____ 189

A Special Dedication
To the Memory of my Parents:
L. Shirley LeVie
and
Donald S. LeVie, Sr.

Acknowledgements

Thanks to my editor
Jaime deBlanc-Knowles, the Association
of Certified Fraud Examiners, and the
countless individuals I have had the
privilege of managing over the years

FROM THE PUBLISHER

Strategic Career Engagement: The Definitive Guide for Getting Hired and Promoted from Donn LeVie Jr. is the natural follow-up book project to his award-winning *Confessions of a Hiring Manager Rev. 2.0* (Second Edition), which was the Winner of the 2012 International Book Award and 2012 Global eBook Award for Jobs/Careers. *Strategic Career Engagement* continues in this vein for shaping a successful vocation path for employees, contractors, and consultants.

In *Strategic Career Engagement*, former Fortune 500 hiring manager, consultant, speaker, and award-winning author Donn LeVie Jr. shows how a successful job- or career-search strategy builds on an existing professional brand. That brand conveys an attitude of serving as the hiring manager's problem solver, solutions provider, and game changer who understands, anticipates, and responds to the hiring manager's business needs at every stage of the hiring process— right up to when the offer is made.

The current offering of career books provides advice from a smorgasbord of experts: a dating specialist/TV celebrity, psychologists and personality professionals, Wall Street marketing executives, a millennial generation career expert, career coaches, and others from different professions and holding a variety of certifications, some of which actually require some experience with hiring, interviewing, and managing people; some demand only completion of web-based training and testing.

Strategic Career Engagement, just like its predecessor, *Confessions of a Hiring Manager Rev. 2.0,* comes from Donn's twenty-five year career reviewing over one thousand cover letters and résumés, conducting hundreds of job interviews, and hiring/managing countless scientific, technical, marketing, and communications professionals for a variety of positions. Over his career, Donn has compiled, categorized, and augmented those approaches candidates have taken that consistently win favor with hiring managers.

Strategic Career Engagement reveals the tactics of a proven action plan designed to shorten the time necessary to get hired or promoted by focusing and reinforcing *your* unique competitive advantages. In today's competitive job market, a personal strategy for developing your career is a must. Without it, you're likely to become just part of someone else's plan to develop their own.

Kings Crown Publishing

INTRODUCTION

Some people change jobs and careers with intent and purpose;
others have it thrust upon them.
The Author

Strategic Career Engagement is about developing a strategy for eliminating the competition for any job or promotion by making your expertise and the benefits of that expertise so much in demand by a hiring manager that you become the only logical choice of candidate. The book is a further development of the "Stacking the Deck" and "Talent Spotting" seminars I present to audiences around the country.

The strategies in this book will work for anyone seeking an internal position with a current employer, an external position with a different employer, or a different career path altogether. Creating a professional brand, building a résumé of achievements that spotlights your expertise, selling yourself in job interviews as a solver of other people's problems — all of that and more gets the attention of a hiring manager, whether that manager sits in an office three floors above where you now work or three time zones away in a different company.

My previous book, *Confessions of a Hiring Manager Rev. 2.0 (Second Edition)*, outlines in detail how to craft cover letters and résumés that get a hiring manager's attention, how to own the job interview, how to stay at the top of the hiring manager's short list long after interviews have concluded, and much more. In *Strategic Career Engagement,* I have augmented and fortified many of the strategies discussed in *Confessions of a Hiring Manager Rev. 2.0.*

1

How can you gain an advantage in the hiring process for your next job or step in your career? Beyond marrying the boss's son or daughter, it sounds like a long shot, but it's easier than you think if you know and apply strategies and tactics that work toward that end.

Three decades in various hiring manager positions as well as my own experiences changing jobs and careers have shown me what works — and what doesn't — when it comes to getting a job offer.

Being able to clearly communicate, verbally and in writing, your value and expertise is essential to progressing in your career; yet countless individuals who are otherwise highly qualified fail miserably because they don't understand the subtle and not-so-subtle human factors involved in the hiring process. The hiring process is as much about establishing personal connections and relationships as it is about your qualified expertise for the position.

Strategic Career Engagement shows you the veritable "mindfield" of challenges you may face in getting to the next round of the hiring process.

- Part I (Chapters 1 – 4) makes you aware of the motivations, prejudices, and presuppositions that influence how hiring managers evaluate potential candidates, and the variables that weigh on the decision to either send them on to the next stage in the hiring process — or not.

- Part II (Chapters 5 – 8) shows you how to shape a portfolio of supportive documentation that addresses a hiring manager's motivations, some of which may not align with the needs of the business. You'll also learn how to stage the release of individual portfolio elements throughout the hiring process that attest to your past ability to perform and promote your potential for future/ongoing success.

- Part III (Chapters 9—11) shows you how to "maximize mind time" by developing a strategy known as *impression management*, which creates and solidifies so-called *associative models* in the minds of hiring managers that build your case as the preferred candidate throughout the entire hiring process.

- Part IV (Chapters 12—14) addresses three important topics that most other career strategy books avoid: (1) making the jump from the public sector to the private sector, and vice-versa; (2) knowing when it's time to leave a job; and (3) becoming an in-demand authority.

An important part of getting hired is understanding the role your *likeability factor* plays in the hiring process. There are two very important variables to getting a job offer: (1) how well your value (the benefits of your expertise, accomplishments) addresses the hiring manager's issues and needs, and (2) the strength of the *continuum of belief* you establish with the hiring manager as you proceed through the hiring process. You'll learn how to create and adjust your likeability factor to the demands of the position and the hiring manager.

In addition, I'll show you how your cover letter can convert features of your past *experience* into future benefits of your *expertise*. You'll also learn how to convert those ordinary duties and responsibilities on your résumé into *core competencies and functional expertise* that put you at the top of the hiring manager's short list.

I'll share with you a post-interview technique that continues to promote your brand and name by building on "associative models" in the minds of hiring managers to become their preferred candidate of choice.

As you begin to create your unique advantage, your job and career strategy will likewise undergo a transformation. Some of these strategies and tactics may require a slight or major adjustment to suit your particular industry, profession, or job. That's OK; the overall

3

intent is to show you a process for how your expertise can and will help solve other people's problems. After all, *creating that unique advantage is really about demonstrating that you are the best candidate for solving other people's problems.*

Before going forward, keep this in mind: Regardless of how renowned your expertise, impressive your cover letter and résumé, or robust the state of the economy, there are always factors beyond your control that determine whether you receive a job interview or even a job offer. *Strategic Career Engagement* focuses on maximizing those elements that are in your control and exerting an influence on those that are not. This approach, in turn, results in a fundamental shift in how you approach your career development.

So, if I see you at an airport, at a conference, or in a restaurant, don't be surprised if I walk up and ask: "What did you do *today* to create that unique advantage for your career advancement?"

Be prepared!

ONE: THE HIRING MANAGER'S SIDE OF THE DESK

Good economy or bad economy, there will always be tough competition for the best-paying jobs and careers. It is especially difficult for people who don't grasp the entirety of the hiring process and fail to develop adequate strategies to see them through the various stages of candidate screening and selection. More often than not, people assume that the act of formulating a *career strategy* that includes a cover letter and résumé is a reaction to a job loss. However, formulating an effective career strategy involves proactive planning in advance of an actual job loss or career shift.

It also involves understanding the point of view of hiring managers. Many hiring managers have difficulty fully assessing an individual's ability for on-the-job success and determining which candidate offers the best all-around package of hard and soft skills for creating and adding value to the team, business unit, or company.

Additionally, hiring managers are under ever-increasing pressure to do a better job of finding fully capable candidates for open positions, partly due to the expense involved with hiring. On average, the cost to hire an employee has jumped by nearly $1,000 since 2012.[1] Hiring

---

[1] SHRM Customized Benchmarking Service

managers are being challenged to more proficiently select candidates who have the highest probability of on-the-job success and to do it more quickly (i.e., cheaply). Thus, it's not always the most qualified individual who receives the job offer; it's often the candidate who makes a lasting personal and professional impression throughout the hiring process.

Speaking for a moment as a hiring manager, becoming *my* candidate of choice is not a matter of luck; it involves understanding *my* main motivation, which is to identify a candidate with a record of demonstrated — and where possible, *quantified* — accomplishments, which are strong indicators for future success in the position. It involves understanding that previous duties/responsibilities are of a lesser concern to *me* — unless those duties and responsibilities can be expressed as benefits of an expertise that led to valuable, higher-order strategic results for former employers. It means having some knowledge of *my* challenges, concerns, and expectations. And it means an awareness and understanding of *my* presuppositions, prejudices, and human factors that may come into play for evaluating potential short list candidates.

The job- or career-search strategy you employ must build on an existing professional brand that conveys to *me* an attitude of serving as *my* problem solver, solutions provider, and game changer who understands, anticipates, and responds to *my* business needs at every stage of the hiring process. In essence, the hiring process is always about *me* and what *I* (i.e., the team, the company) need, and never about *you*.

Becoming the hiring manager's candidate of choice requires a basic understanding of an important marketing principle: What successfully connects the person with a need to the person who can fulfill that need is *value*. It's the same whether you are selling vacuum cleaners, cars, or your professional expertise. If the person with the need perceives and believes that you offer real value, you have fulfilled that need and can make the sale.

The elements of the value you provide form a *continuum of belief* that strengthens your position as you move through the hiring process. As the hiring manager begins an assessment of your value through a cover letter and résumé, he or she begins the journey on the continuum of belief. Your value grows as you proceed to the interview stage and the hiring manager moves forward on the continuum of belief in that value you can provide. This relationship is illustrated in Figure 1.

Figure 1. Relationship Between Your Value and the Continuum of Belief with Hiring Managers

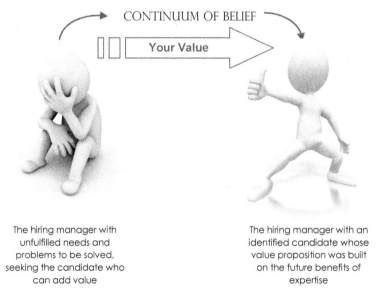

The hiring manager with unfulfilled needs and problems to be solved, seeking the candidate who can add value

The hiring manager with an identified candidate whose value proposition was built on the future benefits of expertise

Your accomplishments, skills, and expertise attest to your value when you communicate how their benefits address the hiring manager's issues.

However, there's so much more you need to know about the hiring manager's world that will help you create that unique advantage over other qualified individuals. The following chapter will delve deeper into the hiring manager's perspective, so that you, the job candidate, can better address his or her needs with your unique advantage.

TWO: THE HIRING MANAGER'S DILEMMA

Everyone is telling the job seeker about how to prepare for the interview, but who is telling the employer? I have wasted countless hours of my time interviewing with employers who don't have a clue as to what they are looking for.

Post from the *HBR Blog Network*,
"Prepare for an Interview by Thinking Like an Employer"

Fifty-three years ago, Douglas McGregor wrote in *The Human Side of Enterprise*: "Behind every managerial decision or action are assumptions about human nature and human behavior." Those assumptions McGregor references are a necessity when hiring managers must evaluate a handful of knowns and a boxcar full of unknowns to predict the future success of a potential employee. It is never as simple or easy as just reviewing a résumé, performing background and reference checks, and conducting an interview.

Human factors serve as a double-edged sword of sorts because they can both help and hinder a hiring decision that selects the best candidate for the position. Various objective assessments are available to help hiring managers evaluate potential candidates, but the use of intuition and other subjective means cannot be ignored in the process — nor can they be elevated above any objective assessment. They are simply tools in the hiring manager's toolbox.

Many human resource professionals and hiring managers believe that hiring failures (hiring the wrong candidates) are a result of some shortcoming in the assessment process; yet, assessing and selecting the right candidate for the position involves substantial *irreducible unpredictability*. We simply cannot and will not accurately predict the future success of any candidate at the time of hire, because our prediction is based on limited historical data provided by the candidate — some of which might not be totally valid. Therefore, the hiring manager cannot eliminate all the unknowns surrounding his or her ability to predict a candidate's future success.

Despite the research that demonstrates the validity of properly used objective assessment tools, many companies, human resource professionals, and hiring managers tend to give more weight to intuition and subjective methods when making a final hiring decision, even though research data suggests that intuitive expertise is a myth.[2] Regardless, this is an area of opportunity for any job seeker as long as hiring managers continue to rely more on gut instinct and intuition, particularly when applicants are aware that hiring managers want solutions providers, game changers, and MacGyver-like problem solvers.

It's been my experience that most qualified candidates fail to anticipate the hiring manager's perspective on the available position. At the same time, hiring managers often rely a bit too much on a candidate's *experience* (what was done) instead of the candidate's *expertise* (how it was done). This miscommunication creates a disengagement that is termed *the job market disconnect*.

The job market disconnect also extends to candidates who think: "If I can just get an interview, I know I can sell myself," much the way some young brides think the wedding is all about the dress. The important part of the relationship (for both the hiring manager and

---

[2] Highhouse, Scott. "Stubborn reliance on intuition and subjectivity in employee selection," *Industrial and Organizational Psychology* (2008), 1, 333–342.

candidate, and the bride and groom) comes after the ceremony (getting hired). No doubt some of this disconnect can be attributed to job descriptions that are not sufficiently specific, that describe prerequisites and duties in too formal or clinical language, that do not convey a sense of the corporate culture, or that simply fail to fully disclose any challenging tasks or responsibilities.

Perhaps the model for clarity in written job postings is one rumored to have been written by Antarctic explorer Sir Ernest Shackleton (1874–1922), who quickly got to the point:

> *Men wanted for hazardous journey. Low wages, bitter cold, long hours of complete darkness. Safe return doubtful. Honour and recognition in event of success.*

A good job description leaves nothing to conjecture as to the skills, knowledge, and expertise the position requires of candidates.

Who and What Is a "Hiring Manager"?

The manager with hiring responsibility has a multifaceted role in the hiring process: first as corporate diplomat who presents the face of the company to applicants; second, as an assessor/investigator of an applicant's character, credibility, technical competence, formal education, honors/awards, and publications; and third, as a prognosticator who predicts a candidate's motivations, cultural fit (a critical variable), and on-the-job success based on a limited set of data that might or might not accurately reflect the candidate's capability and proficiency.

Rare is the individual who has "hiring manager" listed as a title on his or her business card. Being a hiring manager is a responsibility that often accompanies individuals who manage teams or projects, and who must define, initiate, and participate in the hiring process as necessary. Often, the need for additional employees must first reach critical mass before the company sets aside revenue for hiring. It's just as easy for the finance people to tighten the purse strings when there is a vacancy on a team, which then forces the remaining employees to pick up the slack. Been there; done that.

In other words, the manager likely has had to deal with a manpower shortage long before approval and budget was granted to hire additional employees. In the middle of trying to do more with less-than-adequate resources (insufficient project budgets or headcount), the manager must also carve out time for résumé screening, candidate interviews, and post-interview evaluations to determine who receives the job offer.

Most of the time, the manager is also tasked with managing stakeholders at all levels of the organization, addressing issues impacting project deliverables, seeing to customer concerns, and handling matters that concern individual team members. Companies invest significant financial resources to help groom managers to better respond to these and many other events that can impact revenue.

However, despite the various skills and personality assessments available for use during the hiring process, every hiring manager brings to the table prejudices, presuppositions, and expectations that further complicate the process of hiring the best candidate for the position. *Additionally, arriving at a hiring decision is a prediction rife with uncertainty about a candidate's qualifications to succeed in the position because it is a decision based on a limited set of data.*

Add to the stress of that statement the fact that the cost of hiring failures is estimated to be between 1.5 to 5 times the annual cost of the employee. Table 1 shows just some of the associated costs of making the wrong hiring decision.

Table 1. Costs Associated with Hiring Failures

Lost productivity	Separation pay	Separation processing
Accrued vacation	Continued benefits	Advertising/job posts

Recruiting time	Recruiting fee	Interviewing time
Assessment cost/time	Reference check	Criminal check
Credit check	Drug test	Relocation expenses
Temporary contract fee	Orientation	Training
Customer issues from turnover	Potential customer loss from turnover	Possible negligent hiring litigation costs

Hiring the Wrong Employee: Why It Happens

When asked by researchers why a hiring decision didn't work out, hiring managers admitted to shortcomings on their part (listed here in decreasing number of responses):[3]

- Hiring procedures that were not sufficiently rigorous, especially regarding reference checks and interviewing techniques
- Insufficient attention to determining job requirements
- Time constraints
- Insufficient applicant pool
- Not being sufficiently selective
- Inexperience with interviewing applicants (poor judge of ability or character)

Hiring managers pointed out shortcomings with applicants as well (listed here in decreasing order of responses):

- Misrepresentation during interviews or on résumé
- Personality conflict
- Inability to separate personal life issues from job performance
- Technically unqualified for the position

---

[3] Nowicki, Margaret and Joseph Rosse. "Managers' Views of How to Hire: Building Bridges Between Science and Practice," Journal of Business and Psychology, Vol. 17, No. 2, 2002, pp. 157–170.

Hiring the Right Employee: Why It Happens

The same group of managers was asked to describe a successful hiring decision. They attributed these successful decisions to their own intuition, instinct, and luck, as well as an increased thoroughness of reference checks, more rigorous interviews, and more time allowed for the hiring process. Interestingly, 29 percent of the responses cited the applicant's personality or character as contributing to a successful hiring decision, followed by the applicant's experience, education, and communication skills.

Why Hiring Managers Are Often Hesitant Participants in the Hiring Process

Most hiring managers I have known throughout my thirty-year career were at times reluctant players in the hiring process, even though they knew they would benefit from the outcome. There are several key reasons for their hesitation to get involved.

- Most have little formal hiring training.
- Résumé screening and candidate interviews remove hiring managers (and perhaps members of their team) from working on revenue-generating projects.
- They believe (and are often correct in this belief) that the résumé-screening-to-job-offer process is too long, sometimes resulting in losing a highly qualified candidate to a more nimble competitor who is quicker with a job offer.
- They have been overexposed to poorly written résumés, résumés that lack the prerequisites for the position, or cover letters that fail to grab their interest.

It can be difficult to provide productive training on candidate-evaluation methods and tools for a process that is performed only on occasion as demand dictates. Hiring managers and perhaps their teams have performance reviews based on projects that contribute to revenue for the business unit or company, so the training for an infrequent event may be difficult to justify. A lengthy hiring process can result in a company extensively vetting top candidates, only to lose them to competitors who are quicker to present a job offer (or that present a better one).

Hiring Managers' Prejudices and Presuppositions

The majority of candidates who apply for a job never get called for an interview. The exclusion/selection process goes beyond what information is found in a cover letter, a job application, or a résumé. Although there are many ways that candidates can sabotage their job-search efforts, there are instances where being excluded from an interview and a job is beyond the control of the candidate — despite having an impeccable résumé, credentials, and personality. While economic and political factors influence the hiring process to varying degrees, the human factor also plays an important role.

There is no denying that we all bring certain prejudices and presuppositions to any interpersonal interactions. It's no different for hiring managers. Some of these prejudices are overt and some fall below the hiring manager's conscious awareness, yet — despite the extent of their visibility — they do play an influential role in selecting a candidate.

In a university-sponsored study, hiring managers were given 100 random, blind interview evaluations that came from a group consisting of 30 engineers and 70 lawyers. The hiring managers were asked to determine whether a statement similar to the one below referred to an engineer or a lawyer:

He shows some interest in political issues; active in social causes and spends most of his free time on his many hobbies, which include chess, bike riding, and Internet gaming.

Most of the hiring managers in this research study asserted that the statement described an engineer applicant. However, they ignored the fact that, when the description was selected at random, they had a 7 in 10 chance of reading a description about a lawyer.

Whenever I present this example as a group exercise in workshops and seminars, people base their selection on the personality characteristics they associate with each profession. While many, if not most, believed the statement described a lawyer, their reasoning revealed that people usually make predictions and evaluate situations by determining how "typical" the event is given the specific scenario. Not once have I heard someone from the audience justify their selection based on the 70 percent mathematical probability that the description was that of a lawyer.

Prejudices and presuppositions guide our reasoning more than we suppose—and hiring managers are no different than the rest of us.

Positive Prejudice

Positive prejudice is the term given to a situation that occurs when a candidate receives a job offer because he or she most closely aligns with the hiring manager's stereotype of someone in that role and context. It is *not* that the manager dislikes the candidate who fails to align with that imagined employee prototype, but more that he values his perceptions of how well the individual fits the model.

The best available candidate might not necessarily look like the candidate the hiring manager had in mind (or the last person who had the job).

The Bully Mindset

On-the-job bullying (also called *psychological harassment*) can rear its ugly head in many ways but a bully mindset expressed during the hiring process, though not a common occurrence, can prevent qualified candidates from being fairly and completely evaluated.

A study by the Workplace Bullying Institute (WBI) concluded that, while bullying takes place in all ranks within organizations, the vast majority of perpetrators are bosses, managers, supervisors, and executives.

The bully mindset can manifest itself as an extreme form of positive prejudice. For example, the hiring manager might believe that certain positions for which he or she has to interview and subsequently manage do not warrant the required effort or attention. The problem becomes exacerbated later when a hiring manager sees no value of a particular position despite the organization's need for it. That reluctant attitude is one that comes through during interviews, no matter how well the hiring manager attempts to disguise it.

I once worked in an organization where the division general manager was fairly vocal about his preference not to "waste headcount" (as he called it) on permanent technical writer positions. He would have preferred to use the available requisitions to hire more engineers or technical marketing professionals, and only use technical writing contractors on an "as needed" basis.

Every 15–18 months, I had to provide a written justification for this personality-challenged division manager to maintain the headcount on my small team of technical writers and editors. This effort unnecessarily elevated stress levels for everyone involved, despite the fact that the business unit placed a high value on the technical publications function and its contributions to the company's strategic objectives.

Excluding the Tails

Let's get mathematical for a moment. In any statistical distribution, the *tails* (extremes) of a bell curve represent data (people, objects, or information) that lie on the farthest sides of a normal distribution of that data (generally beyond the second or third standard deviation). When assessing typical elements of a population, the data under the tails are often disregarded. See Figure 2 for a graphic representation of a normal distribution, standard deviations, and tails.

Figure 2. Normal Distribution and Standard Deviations

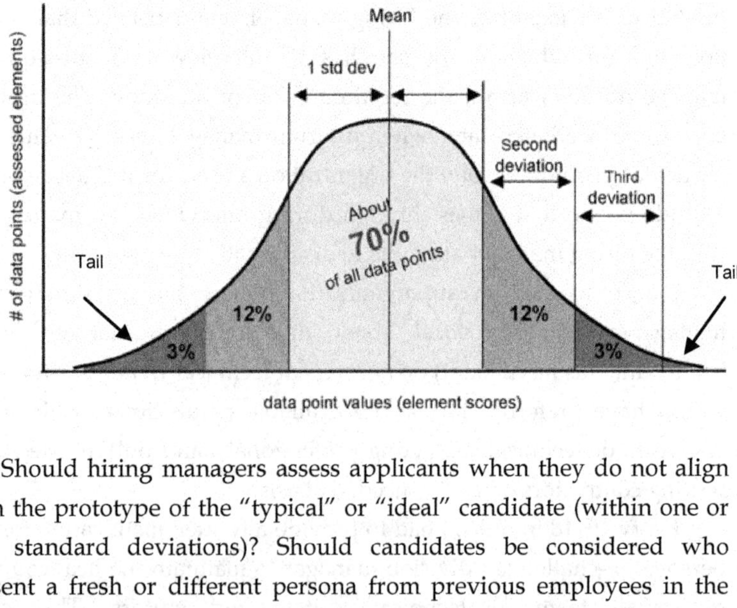

Should hiring managers assess applicants when they do not align with the prototype of the "typical" or "ideal" candidate (within one or two standard deviations)? Should candidates be considered who present a fresh or different persona from previous employees in the position (that is, candidates who fall under the tails of the normal distribution)?

Let's consider some normal statistics for NBA players. Eighty percent of NBA players are black; the average height is 6' 7"; the average weight is 225 lbs. Do we exclude Asian and white players because they lie outside the normal distribution? If so, we miss out on such outstanding players as Jeremy Lin, Yao Ming, John Havlicek, and Larry Bird.

Do we exclude all players who are shorter than 6'7" because they are outside the normal distribution? If so, we miss out on Tyrone "Muggsy" Bogues, who at 5'3" enjoyed a successful NBA career.

Do we exclude players who are heavier than 225 lbs. because they are outside the normal distribution? If so, we miss out on Shaquille O'Neal, who tipped the scales at a svelte 340 lbs.

Objective Assessment Tools: How Valid and Useful Are They for Hiring Decisions?

The four-year college degree was once the ticket to any good-paying career. Today, however, companies are using innovative methods for screening all types of job applicants, from live customer-support simulations during interviews, to using the profiles of high performers as weighted factors for evaluating potential new hires from further consideration. Such a process tends to be self-improving as data accumulates, resulting in a periodic raising of the bar for future candidates. If a candidate has a criminal record, credit report, GPA, or SAT score, it's likely an employer is using such data as additional pre-screen tools.

There's a rapidly growing interest and belief among employers today that data analytics can be used to remove the gut instinct factor from the hiring process. In fact, 26 percent of U.S. employers used pre-hire assessments in 2001; by 2013, that number jumped to 57 percent, reflecting the need to better identify quality candidates.

University of Chicago economist Steven Davis discovered that the labor market churn of hires and separations had dropped by more than 25 percent since 2000, indicating an improvement in upfront screening of candidates who will remain on the job longer.

At the same time, this increased use of pre-hire assessments makes it more difficult for recent college graduates and long-term unemployed folks to find a job, particularly when pre-hire assessments include situational interviews where a candidate may not have the specific experience or contextual knowledge to draw upon.

Several studies of hiring manager presuppositions reveal that hiring managers believe objective testing measures are not worthwhile. However, a fairly substantial body of research demonstrates the usefulness of candidate testing. Candidate testing, when properly administered, can greatly assist in making successful hiring choices. Important criteria for objective testing of candidates include the cost of tool development and implementation, the validity of the test in predicting work outcomes, ease of test administration, and several other factors. However, an objective assessment that fails to provide high levels of validity results in poor hiring decisions and ultimately higher costs due to hiring the wrong employee.

A recent *New York Times* article cited a paper by researchers published in the Proceedings of the National Academy of Sciences who used a computer program to assess subjects' personalities based on Facebook "Likes."[4] To measure the model's ability to predict accurately, researchers compared its verdicts to subjects' ratings of their own personalities. The results showed that given a sufficient number of "Likes," the computer did very well at judging people's personalities — better than the subjects' friends or coworkers.

Using a five personality dimension model (see the "Big 5" Personality Dimensions in the next chapter for details), the program did as good a job assessing subjects as their spouses did. In addition,

---

[4] North, Anna. "How Your Facebook Likes Could Cost You a Job," *The New York Times*, January 20, 2015.

researchers also investigated the program's ability to predict 13 "life outcomes" that are tied to personality, including health, political affiliations, and general life satisfaction. The model on which the program was based did a better job predicting 12 of the 13 outcomes (life satisfaction prediction was the exception).

Even more interesting was the model's ability to do a better job than the subjects' self-ratings on predicting four outcomes: Facebook use; number of Facebook friends; use of alcohol, tobacco, and drugs; and field of study.

This research has important implications for data analysis playing a more comprehensive role in the hiring process, particular in the upfront candidate screening process. Currently, many hiring managers use social media posts, blogs, and inappropriate photos as a process for excluding candidates from further consideration for open positions. Now there might be a way to predict a candidate's propensity for tobacco or drug use long before the post-interview trip to the clinic for a toxicology screen.

While such Facebook-based data analytics can present privacy concerns, soon hiring managers may have access to a tool that helps them better assess more obscure facets of a candidate's social media persona that may — or may not — allow them to continue forward in the hiring process.

Until that methodology becomes a reality, there's another computer application that's been in use for over twenty years to prescreen job candidate résumés: the job bot.

Job Bots: One Possible Reason You Didn't Get the Job

Not all résumés get an initial screening by hiring managers or recruiters. Once the dumping ground for solicited and unsolicited résumés and job applications, many big company HR departments have been forced to devote more resources to employment law and related legislation; implementing the Affordable Care Act; and employee benefit packages. As a result, many HR departments are turning to résumé- and job-application screening software to handle the overwhelming number of such documents they receive. It's a good idea to know how these systems (called *applicant tracking systems* or ATSs) work so you can make your résumé more relevant to the job for which you're applying.

Most of these systems incorporate a specific software application called a *bot*. A bot (Internet-speak for *robot*) is an automated application used to perform simple and repetitive tasks that would be time-consuming, mundane, or impossible for a human to perform. Bots can be used for productive tasks, but they are also frequently used for malicious purposes, such as identity theft or to launch denial of service attacks.

Job bots are software applications embedded in applicant tracking systems used by HR departments or third-party providers since the late 1990s to screen pools of online applications and online résumé submissions. As far back as 2001, some job bots were able to search 300,000 résumés in ten seconds. The federal government uses the Resumix system to screen online applications and résumés. Resumix and other such job bots filter these documents through tens or hundreds of thousands of *Knowledge-Skill-Ability* terms (called KSAs) to determine whether an application or résumé meets the essential and preferable skills for a particular job vacancy.

The automated application-résumé screening process is designed to reject as many unqualified applications as possible. If you've ever been surprised (or angry) when you received a rejection letter stating that you "did not have the required minimum experience or skills," even though you may have worked in an identical position for years, it's likely you were the victim of a job bot. The job bot in the application tracking system is programmed to look for specific information (job

22

title, functional skills, years of experience). If you do not format your experience in the expected manner, then, as far as the job bot is concerned, it doesn't exist.

How Job Bots Work

Here's a brief overview of how the job bot software analyzes your résumé.

1. HR receives your résumé (along with hundreds of others).

2. Your résumé is run through a computer program called a *parser*, which removes styling and formatting (bold typeface, underlining, bullets, etc.), and separates text into recognizable strings of characters for additional analysis.

3. The parser assigns meaning and context to résumé content, separating phrases into information types, such as contact information, functional skills, experience, education, language skills, etc.

4. Employer uses key words to search candidates; matching terms are searched from the results collected in Step 3.

5. Your résumé is scored based on relevancy, which is the semantic matching of employer search terms and your experience.

6. (Optional): If your résumé makes it this far, it may be further "filtered" by persons who may or may not be familiar with your specific, unique knowledge or expertise. In such cases, these individuals are instructed to forward your résumé to a higher-level reviewer to determine whether it should be sent on to a hiring manager. This is the weakest link in the chain. I don't know about you, but leaving that decision in the hands of an unknown person makes me just a bit nervous.

Structuring your résumé really does require some forethought and a distinctive writing style to overcome the barriers presented by these job bots. A résumé that is not optimized for ATSs and job bots risks never being viewed by human eyes.

More Bad News About Job Bots

According to a 2012 *CIO* magazine article, job bots are error-prone apps that eliminate "75 percent of job-seekers' chances of landing an interview as soon as they submit their résumés, no matter how qualified they may be."[5] Peter Cappelli, author of *Why Good People Can't Get Jobs* states that job bots are inexpensive but "not very effective in finding the people companies want."[6]

Job bot accuracy depends on the decision rules used in parsing applications and résumés, which in turn depends on the quality and extent of research performed to determine appropriate KSAs for a particular function or position.

While the "scrubbing" of applications and résumés by many ATSs can remove potential bias (e.g., age, gender, and ethnicity), it's possible that information linked to these factors may not be ignored.

Another problem is that humans can spot talent better than any software algorithm, and this is especially true as more fields become technology-driven, and the types and degrees of specialization require a trained eye to spot. According to an HR acquaintance, "A great résumé gets noticed, but at most companies it's about who referred you."

---

[5] Levinson, Meredith. "5 Insider Secrets for Beating Applicant Tracking Systems," *CIO*, March 1, 2012, http://tinyurl.com/kswlm5a.)
[6] Capelli, Peter. *Why Good People Can't Get Jobs*, (Wharton Digital Press, 2012).

Getting Past the Job Bots

The goal is to get your résumé past the job-bot gatekeepers and low-level human screeners, and into the hands of a hiring manager. Here are some techniques for getting your résumé past ATSs and job bots:

1. Don't just focus on the words in the job description. Read the description carefully to identify underlying themes, repeated phrases, and jargon; key words are not always obvious. Without the right key words (or enough of them), your résumé will likely be rejected. It's also important to use proper key word placement and frequency to maximize their value. Try mirroring where you think covert key word placement appears in the job ad, and the frequency of key word usage.

2. Stay focused on what's important to the person reviewing (or the job bot scanning) the résumé. Avoid additional irrelevant information that can distract from the position requirements, as this can result in a rejection. Don't list coursework in lieu of required certifications, degrees, or licenses. Don't list out-of-date or irrelevant professional designations.

3. Prioritize the words on a résumé. The *Résumé Help* blog (www.resume-help.org) recommends analyzing the job description to build a list of priority and secondary words. Priority résumé key words are those used in the job title, used in description headlines, or used more than twice. Secondary résumé key words make mention of competitor companies or brand-name experience, key word phrases, and notable industry qualifications (special certifications, designations, etc.).

4. Consult an insider for help finding relevant words for a position of interest. Use your LinkedIn network to find (or connect) with someone in an industry group forum who can help with this.

5. Pepper all job-related words across your résumé. Screeners factor in depth of expertise (e.g., years of experience); use the same job-related words on your résumé as the ones that appear in the job ad. Order bullet list items in descending order of relevancy to the job description.

6. Create a relevant category expertise section near the top one-third of the first page of the résumé. Populate this table with relevant generic category expertise (e.g., finance, accounting, operations, audit, investigation, etc.). Specific category expertise could include descriptors such as *risk management, financial transactions and fraud schemes, fraud prevention and deterrence, construction fraud, Medicare/Medicaid fraud, data analytics,* etc.

So, what are the chances your résumé will be evaluated by a job bot? That depends on the size of the company with the open position, whether that company is using a third-party agency to screen résumés, and the specific position for which you are applying. And it's important to understand that making it past the job-bot gauntlet only gets you to the next step in the hiring process: the job interview. That's it. The skills needed for the job interview, and ultimately receiving a job offer, involve other factors.

If you receive an email response immediately after submitting your résumé, then it's likely it's already been rejected. Continue tweaking your résumé and resubmitting until you don't get the immediate response. When that happens, there's a good chance that your résumé made it past the first hurdle and may be in the hands a human being and not a software "terminator."

What's in a Name?

The names we were given at birth have a significant impact on how we are viewed and sometimes accepted by others. Recent research suggests that our names also influence how we are perceived by hiring managers, recruiters, and human resource professionals. In some instances, your name can either help or hurt your job chances.

People like what is familiar and similar to them; they are particularly partial to people with similar values, personalities, and demographic backgrounds. Additionally, research has demonstrated that unique names (unusual names or unique spellings) suggest less attractive characteristics, and are seen as less desirable, than more ordinary names. People with nicknames were perceived as having less successful characteristics, while males with longer names connoted more ethical concern and more success. Candidates with formal versions of a name (Robert instead of Bob or Bobby; Katherine instead of Kate or Katie) elicit different inferences about personality, while rare names were rated lower in socio-economic status than more common names. These implied characteristics are *perceptions only* — not necessarily reality — but they can be obstacles in the process.

In many instances, race or ethnic origin can be suggested by an applicant's name. Since the early 1970s, African-American parents increasingly chose African-sounding names for their children in order to incorporate a positive, healthy cultural identity, and this pattern continues today. One study found that African-sounding names tend to be more common among African-Americans in lower socio-economic status. However, the same study found that African-sounding names are unrelated to quality of life after considering education, parents' education, age/marital status of mother, and other factors.

What does this mean for job candidates? The results of the study showed how choice of names can, in some professions and careers, influence who gets called for a job interview:

- Résumés with African-sounding names received fewer callbacks than the Caucasian names.

- Higher quality résumés elicited more callbacks with Caucasian names, but the higher quality had no impact on callbacks when paired with an African-sounding name.

In 2004, a *20/20* segment on ABC posted 22 pairs of names with identical names on well-known job websites. Caucasian names received more attention than African-American sounding names. Why did this happen? One theory suggests that individuals resort to "habits of mind" when engaging in much of our behavior—i.e., we make decisions without giving them too much attention. Essentially, there is *no* conscious malice aforethought in such situations; it is more likely a human factor effect.

For résumés that are sent first to human resources, assigning a number or using only the candidate's initials on the résumé, cover letter, or application can help mask ethnic origins or racial makeup, and minimize any subconscious prejudice in those who assess a candidate's overall qualifications for a position. For cover letters and résumés sent directly to hiring managers without human resource filtering of identifying information, it's possible that the hiring manager may assign some value judgment to any ethnic/racial clues from the candidate's name. That's just another one of those inescapable human factors that arise in the hiring process. Human resources must work closely with recruiters and hiring managers to avoid any habits-of-mind situations from occurring during candidate screening.

What About the Ethnicity of the Hiring Manager?

In a similar vein, does the ethnicity of the hiring manager have any influence on the ethnicity of new hires? According to a 2006 study conducted by the Institute for Research on Labor and Employment at UC Berkeley, hiring manager ethnicity plays a significant role in the racial makeup of new hires, though the primary determinants of the degree of the effect are the characteristics of the workplace (blue collar or professional) and the geographic location.

The study showed that whites, Hispanics, and Asian hiring managers hire more whites and fewer blacks than do black managers. These differences are especially pronounced in the South. Where Hispanics constitute at least 30 percent of the local geographic population, Hispanic hiring managers hire more Hispanics and fewer whites than do white managers. In other words, in some regions of the country, managers tend to select candidates along preferred racial lines and that candidates prefer to apply for jobs where hiring managers are of the same race.

The Question of Overqualification

Another potential obstacle in the path to getting hired is a hiring manager's concern for possible overqualification. There is no one definition for what constitutes overqualification, as it varies across companies, industries, and countries. However, a very basic and broad designation would be a candidate who has too much experience, the wrong kind of experience, or a higher level of experience than what the position demands.

The *Scale of Perceived Overqualification*, a self-reporting assessment, also incorporates perceived surpluses in education, experience, knowledge, skills, and abilities. In some circles, even an unrealistic expectation of a starting salary or the nature of the job can induce perceptions of overqualification in the minds of candidates.

Many, if not most, hiring managers have higher expectations of overqualified employees: They tend to ramp up quicker, work harder, show more initiative, and be more effective leaders than those who simply meet job qualifications. The fear about hiring overqualified individuals centers on job dissatisfaction. If no opportunities arise for growth or promotion, the overqualified employee could eventually start underperforming and, eventually, leave the position.

During the worldwide oil crisis of the mid-1980s, downsized oil company geologists flooded environmental sciences companies with résumés and cover letters, hoping to continue their career in the earth sciences (for about one-third to one-half of their previous salaries).

I, too, briefly considered such a move. For most of the available positions, the oil company geologists were overqualified, as many positions involved field monitoring of water quality control wells in remote areas and other similar fieldwork that just didn't task the knowledge expertise of petroleum geologists. Environmental companies were reluctant to hire oil industry refugees because they assumed that, as soon as the price of a barrel of oil returned to the $25–$35 level from the $10 level, the geologists would return to the oil patch.

When I made the transition from the oil and gas exploration profession to software documentation development in 1986, I feared being considered overqualified for any position. I had experience using a variety of complicated software (and writing some simple programs) as an exploration geologist, and was the unofficial division technical editor for professional journal articles and technical papers. My "new" résumé gave more ink to my software skills, managerial experience, and scientific communications expertise, and less to my core geological, geophysical, and geochemical duties, responsibilities, and accomplishments. It took nine months of effort to get a job, but when I did it was with a software development company that created pipeline mapping programs for oil companies.

Referral Hires, Non-Referral Hires, and Internal Hires

There are three ways by which candidates enter the hiring process: as an external candidate, as a referral candidate, or as an internal candidate. In my experience, internal candidates generally enjoy the biggest advantage, followed closely by referral candidates, and then external candidates in a distant third. Somewhere between 33 and 67 percent of jobs found and filled are through personal referrals.

Through personal referrals, much of the uncertainty in the hiring process is reduced or eliminated altogether from the equation, which leads to a higher probability of getting a job offer (and getting it more quickly). It is also a low-cost recruitment tool that hiring managers and human resources like very much. You simply must be strategic in designing and building your internal and external professional networks to increase the probably of being referred for an open position.

The chart in Figure 3 is from a report at SilkRoad (www.silkroad.com) listing the top ten online recruitment marketing sources. From the chart, it appears that Indeed.com is the most popular online recruitment marketing source for interviews; however, Monster.com and "Unspecified Job Board" have the highest interview-to-hire conversion rates.

Figure 3. Top 10 Online Recruitment Marketing Sources

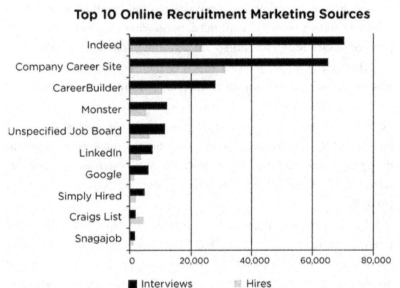

Top 10 Online Recruitment Marketing Sources

Source: SilkRoad

Recruitment Marketing Effectiveness

A 2012 comprehensive study (222,000 job postings, 9.3 million applications, 147,440 interviews, and 94,155 hires) from SilkRoad provides some interesting conclusions about the effectiveness of recruiting:

- External sources (specific job search engines, job boards, print advertising, job fairs) and internal sources (referrals, inside hires, walk-ins, company career sites) result in about the same number of interviews; however, *internal sources produce almost twice the number of hires.*

- Company career sites are the best online recruitment source based on interviews and hires.

- Referrals remain the strongest base for internal recruitment marketing, followed by inside hires and company career sites.
- Job search engines are far more effective than job boards at returning both interviews and hires.

In a landmark study on hiring and social networks (not virtual social networks like Facebook, but social networks that involved face-to-face interactions) conducted by Stanford University in 1996,[7] researchers concluded the following:

- Social networks favorably influence the composition of the pool of job candidates.
- Applicants referred by current employees are more likely to be interviewed and offered jobs than external non-referral candidates.
- Network referrals are advantaged at both the interview and job offer stages compared to external non-referral applicants.

The researchers also determined why referral candidates had such an advantage over non-referral candidates:

- During labor shortages, referrals provide a quick and inexpensive method for generating a pool of applicants that is smaller than the pool generated by job boards or job search engines, thereby increasing employee engagement in the process.
- The "benefit of the doubt" effect creates a tendency for recruiters to give referral candidates the benefit of the doubt during screening, which encourages employees to continue to

---

[7] Fernandez, Roberto *et al* (2006). "Getting a Job: Networks and Hiring in a Retail Bank," Stanford University, pp. 1–47.

recommend referrals, thereby creating a process closed to non-referral candidates (as a side note, the quicker a candidate receives a job offer, the sooner recruiters get paid; therefore, any process that generates job offers/hires more quickly results in the recruiter making more money).

- Social network hiring tends to produce better job description-worker matches than other types of recruitment

Another reason employee referrals are the preferred entry method to jobs is because the average length of employment is greater with referrals than with the other two methods for entering the hiring process, as the chart in Figure 4 reveals.

Figure 4. Length of Employment vs. Types of Hiring

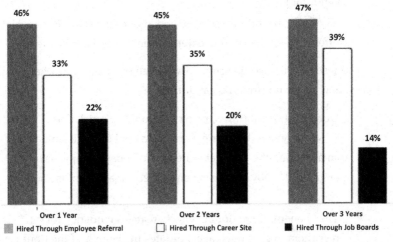

In 2012, one San Jose company of 3,500 employees filled 75 percent of their available positions through external hires. Today, that number is down to 40 percent since recruiters started to "think inside first" when filling positions.

Internal hires retain not only intellectual property knowledge but organizational knowledge, which they can put to use in new roles to ramp up more quickly than external hires.

The website Indeed.com allows users to explore hiring trends and jobs for specific functions and fields. Users can also track the top job trends by key word, geographic market, and industry, as Figure 5 shows.

Figure 5. Indeed.com Screen Showing Searchable Job Trends

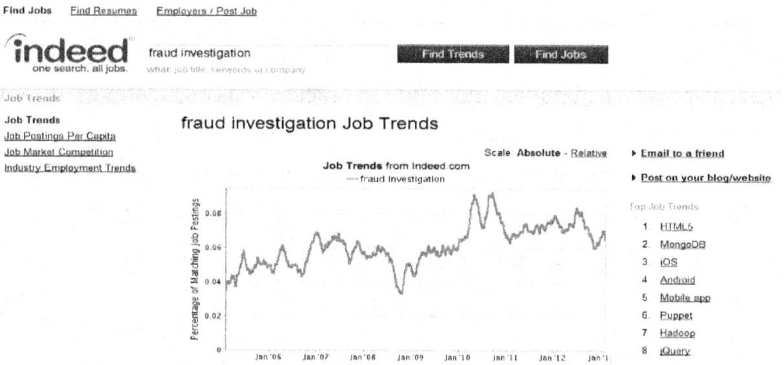

Social Network Sites as an Exclusionary Recruiting Tool

Technology and the rise of social network sites (SNSs) have changed the face of employee recruiting. Research has revealed that corporate Facebook sites receive more hits than the corresponding company websites for job postings. While many companies are now integrating SNSs with traditional recruitment practices (internal job postings, referrals from current employees, etc.), more are using job board sites (Monster.com, Indeed.com, Ladders ,etc.) and, in my opinion, the best SNS for job networking: LinkedIn.

Employers also use SNSs to screen candidates; in fact, use of SNSs for such purposes increased to 37 percent in 2012 compared to 12 percent in 2006, according to a CareerBuilder survey.[8] In 2012, more hiring managers rejected candidates because of the variety of negative information discovered on SNSs, with nearly 50 percent of survey respondents expressing concern about inappropriate photos or information about candidate drug and alcohol use, often conveyed in inappropriate photos.[9]

So, do employers use SNS in recruiting efforts? Yes—not necessarily to locate candidates, but to *exclude* candidates from further consideration because of the posting of questionable content or content that raises issues about a candidate's character. Job candidates of all age groups must scrub all social media content of questionable postings and images. If there's a way to discover it, a hiring manager will find it and use it to eliminate you from consideration for a position. If content in any format doesn't present you in the most favorable professional light, remove it. Hiring managers can easily determine who you are when everyone is looking; what they want to know when making a hiring decision is who you are when no one is watching.

When it comes to using SNSs for job searches or career promotion, less is more. LinkedIn is still by far the best SNS to build a network of valuable contacts and participate in discussions pertinent to career goals. However, SNSs may not be the most effective way to find and secure jobs. Ray Van Es, an HR management advisor and author who lives in Luxembourg, has worked with students and young

---

[8] Grasz, Jennifer. "Thirty-seven percent of companies use social networks to research potential job candidates," CareerBuilder, April 18, 2012, www.careerbuilder.com/share/aboutus/pressreleasesdetail.aspx?id=pr691&sd=4%2F18%2F2012&ed=4%2F18%2F2099.

[9] *Ibid.*, Grasz.

professionals internationally. He has tracked their progress after graduation and discovered some interesting trends:

- Most who are successful and continue being successful are *not* active on the Internet.
- Many do not have a LinkedIn profile, and the ones that do are not very active; social media use is restricted to interacting with a very small group of friends they know personally.
- They are not jumping on SNSs for career purposes, but like to explore career-related apps on smartphones and other devices.
- They build a strong profile (brand) before graduation and continue adding to it once their careers begin.
- They prefer face-to-face networking to virtual networking.

Ray's conclusions about these and other observations may signal a change in approaches to career strategies:

The successful graduates and young professional are applying old career development actions, while enjoying modern [social media] techniques for their personal convenience. In other words: No chaotic (Internet) environment for the successful graduates and young professionals.[10]

Confessions of a Hiring Manager Rev. 2.0 (Second Edition) contains my thoughts on using social media for job and career strategies.

---

[10] Personal correspondence

THREE: RAISE YOUR LIKEABILITY FACTOR

Likeonomics is a term that explains the new affinity economy where the most likeable people, ideas, and organizations are the ones we believe in, buy from, and get inspired by. This connection is apparent in all manners of social, political, commerce, and business relationships, and is especially important in the hiring process.

In a study published in the *Journal of Occupational and Organizational Psychology*, researchers discovered a strong correlation between initial impressions of interviewers and their evaluations of candidate responses to structured interview questions. The initial impressions corresponded with candidate extroversion and verbal skills, with job qualifications being equal.[11] In other words, *favorable first impressions created by candidates during the rapport-building stage of job interviews (that is, small talk) influenced interviewers' subsequent evaluations.*

All skills, knowledge, and experience being equal among candidates, most hiring managers will hire the candidate that makes a memorable impression on a professional *and* personal level. In other words, if you present yourself as a likeable person during the interview, people tend to be more interested in what you have to offer.

---

[11] Barrick, *et al.* "Candidate characteristics driving initial impressions during rapport building: implications for employment interview validity," *Journal of Occupational and Organizational Psychology*, 2012, Vol. 82, No. 2, pp. 330–352.

However, if you do not connect on a personal level—regardless of the value of your skill set—it may be more difficult to get an offer from a hiring manager. Strong interpersonal skills, excellent verbal communication skills, and a friendly personality help set the stage for the hiring manager's receptivity and strengthen that continuum of belief so necessary to continue moving through the hiring process.

At the same, those who hint at being a high-maintenance employee are often the ones who upset an established, positive working team dynamic. Creating rapport and a positive connection is what opens doors for others to see and hear to what you have to offer. If no connection takes place on this level, it is likely your job hunt will continue.

Research has consistently demonstrated that of the "Big Five" Personality Dimensions (*neuroticism, extroversion, openness to experience, agreeableness, conscientiousness*), an applicant's level of extroversion is the best single predictor of whether the individual receives a job offer. A job interview is, after all, a social interaction, and the most salient behaviors exhibited by an applicant in such a situation are his or her social interaction skills.

These skills are critical as hiring manager prejudices, presuppositions, and expectations complicate the decision to hire the best available candidate. As mentioned previously, every hiring decision is a prediction rife with uncertainty that depends on some expectation of future performance.

Strong social interaction skills—along with solid expertise and a list of accomplishments—can go far to minimize these barriers to a job offer. This important chapter will show you how to package your core competencies and functional expertise with a high likeability factor. Getting hired is always about which candidate best responds to the needs of the hiring manager, and not necessarily about the most qualified person.

Every business enterprise recognizes that hiring the right employees is critical for success. For positions that require direct client or customer contact, hiring the right employee is especially important because such individuals represent the boundary between the organization and its client/customer. The behavior of these front-line employees instantly influences customers' perceptions of the quality of service and support. The "hire for attitude, train for skill" mantra is a popular one in many service-related professions.

Even businesses with a large employee population that does not or rarely interacts with customers requires individuals who possess interpersonal skills that allow for productive teamwork, adaptability, and flexibility to changing project directions or leadership. While hiring the right people is an obvious goal, managers do not always make hiring decisions based on the attributes that have been shown to be the best predictors of job performance. If that were the case, then employee turnover and the costs for hiring the wrong people would be lower.

In this chapter, we will look at two of the three components of the hiring process that can be influenced by a candidate's personality and likeability to better improve the odds of receiving a job offer:

1. Intangible, subjective factors that influence hiring manager decisions before, during, and after the interview

2. Subtleties of job interviews as social interaction that can work to the candidate's advantage in continuing on in the hiring process.

The third component consists of a strategy for continuing the *likeability streak* throughout the hiring process as demonstrated in cover letters and résumés and will be addressed in those respective chapters.

41

Challenges and Issues in the Hiring Manager's Domain

One of the major issues confronting the hiring manager over the past several decades has been the inefficiency of the entire hiring process. It is a time-consuming and labor-intensive task, especially with multiple positions to fill. The infusion of both cover letters, résumés (most of which are poorly written, fail to engage the hiring manager's interest, or do not properly promote the candidate's expertise), and job applications can be overwhelming. Manually sorting through a stack of cover letters and résumés is perhaps a hiring manager's least favorite job responsibility, even when assisted by recruiters and job bots.

Hundreds of research studies from more than three decades reveal the presuppositions, prejudices, and preconceived notions many hiring managers bring to the job interview:

- Inclination of interviewers to "rush to judgment" in preliminary interactions with candidates (highlighting the critical importance of the first impression)
- Inability to suppress personal bias and prejudice during job interviews (due in part to human nature)
- Giving more consideration to negative information than positive information about the candidate's skills, knowledge, or experience
- Unawareness of and reluctance to use objective methods for assessing candidate suitability

"Rush to Judgment" in Early Stages of Job Interviews

The manager with hiring responsibility has a multifaceted role in the hiring process: first as corporate diplomat who presents the face of the company to applicants; second, as an assessor/investigator of an applicant's character, credibility, technical competence, formal education, honors/awards, and publications; and third, as a prognosticator who predicts a candidate's motivations, cultural fit (a critical variable), and on-the-job success based on a limited set of data that may or may not accurately reflect the candidate's capability and proficiency.

Hiring managers make assumptions about candidate evaluation approaches. One study reported that 72 percent of hiring managers surveyed indicated that conscientiousness was a better predictor of employee performance than intelligence, when in fact the reverse was true. *Even when presented with evidence of strong correlations between test scores and job performance, many hiring managers preferred the power of intuition and chemistry (that is, the influence of personality and likeability) to hard data and rational arguments as critical factors for candidate selection.*

As mentioned previously, the human factors involved in this multifaceted role can be a double-edged sword, because the presence of these variables can both help and hinder decision making that leads to the selection of the best available candidate. People make initial (visual) category-based judgments of others (the "first impression") before they know anything about the person individually. These initial first impressions can color subsequent assessments of a candidate's more relevant qualities for a particular position.

Such a top-down approach for assessing candidates suggests that a positive or negative stereotype based on an initial impression will cause hiring managers to force-fit subsequent information about the candidate into associations with that stereotype. Corporate training programs from HR can alert hiring managers to such tendencies and help mitigate their influence in the hiring process.

Unsuppressed Personal Bias and Prejudice

Prejudice is often seen as negative. When it is so, it can raise serious legal issues for a company. Unconcealed racism and sexism in organizations is illegal, yet minority and women candidates still face obstacles in the job market through less obvious situations. The Bureau of Labor Statistics reports that minorities and women still find it more difficult to be hired for executive-level positions in corporations, but easily find jobs in roles that are more consistent with stereotypes.

Given equal technical/professional expertise among remaining short-list candidates, hiring managers often ask: "Which candidate would I and my team prefer to work with?" Typically, that response will be the candidate that made the most favorable professional *and* personal impression with the hiring manager and the interview team. As Dale Carnegie wrote in *How Win Friends and Influence People*: "First, arouse in the other person an eager want. He who can do this has the whole world with him. He who cannot walks a lonely way."

The takeaway: *If you don't have a personality, get one – and learn how to manage it.*

Egocentric Bias

Here's a fact of life: it is human nature to believe personal contributions to any team project are greater than they actually are or were. This egocentric bias goes beyond creatively embellishing one's participation or inflating the value of any solution to a problem. In a job interview, it's common to elaborate on an accomplishment because no one else was closer to that effort. However, the greater the psychological distance between you and something you may have only been peripherally involved with, the less vivid those details appear.

Therefore, when asked about past accomplishments in job interviews, there's a tendency for candidates to overestimate the value of any particular individual contribution or effort. But being aware of egocentric bias makes it possible to balance this lopsided perspective with that of fairness for two reasons:

- It helps place our own contributions and those of others in proper perspective because solutions to problems often arise

44

from an "idea soup" (conversations with others, for example) we have been exposed to over time. One great idea is usually the byproduct of many good ones.

- Acknowledging the contributions of others ensures no one is exploited or thrown under the bus for self-serving motivations.

Hiring managers will take favorable notice of candidates who can successfully convey an honest sense of fairness and an appropriate level of egocentric bias during job interviews.

Emphasis on the Negative More Than the Positive

Hiring managers often use some negative aspect of an applicant's background to justify the rejection of a candidate who fails to meet hiring manager stereotypes. This emphasis on the negative is often an extension of positive prejudice — except, in this case, it is overemphasis of some real or perceived *deficiency* (that may or may not be material to the responsibilities and duties of the position) that affects the hiring manager's decision. Overemphasis on the negative is sometimes seen in inexperienced managers during annual reviews or opportunities for promotion whereby one minor disagreement or issue during the year overshadows all the positive contributions a candidate made during the period.

While such situations rarely surface during job interviews with external candidates, they can arise when a candidate is interviewing for an internal promotion or new position. If a candidate is asked to explain the negative situation to an internal hiring manager, his or her best defense should be immediately admitting to any wrongdoing without throwing any other parties under the bus. Such a tactic highlights personal integrity and honesty. Clergyman John Maxwell wrote that an individual must be big enough to admit to mistakes, smart enough to profit from them, and strong enough to correct them.

Reluctance to Use Objective Methods for Assessing Candidate Suitability

In a 2011 study by Cornell University,[12] researchers wanted to know the relative emphasis hiring managers placed on *general mental abilities* (GMA) and the different dimensions of personality: *agreeableness, conscientiousness, emotional stability, extroversion,* and *openness to experience* in assessing employment suitability. To answer this question, researchers used a host of high-powered analytical tools.

The cluster analyses revealed that some groups of managers might be making better hiring decisions in practice than others. However, the research also showed that, while overall GMA had been consistently demonstrated to be the strongest predictor of job performance, it was not highly valued by managers in the study. Three of the Big 5 personality dimensions were consistently emphasized more: *agreeableness, conscientiousness,* and *emotional stability,* with *conscientiousness* being the strongest predictor of performance. The takeaway: *If you don't have a personality, get one – and learn how to manage it.*

At different times in a candidate's career, the GMA dimension may take higher precedence as roles and responsibilities increase and duties change, but this limited study reveals that *despite the objective criteria used to evaluate potential candidates, likeability/personality – along with a mix of hiring manager presuppositions, intuitive assessment, and subjective criteria – often plays the major role in candidate selection.*

Another possible reason hiring managers are reluctant to place much faith in objective assessment tools is because much of the

---

[12] Tews, Michael, Kathryn Stafford, and J. Bruce Tracey. "What Matters Most? The Perceived Importance of Ability and Personality for Hiring Decisions," *Cornell Hospitality Quarterly,* Vol. 52, No. 2, 2011, pp. 94–101.

research into recruiting and candidate selection is performed by academics in industrial and organizational psychology. Their conclusions about the validity, objective assessment, and prediction of work outcomes are sometimes based on arcane terminology, a very small population segment (or in subjects in controlled laboratory conditions), and advanced statistical measures, the details of which are beyond the understanding of most hiring managers and other mere mortals. While validity coefficients, F-statistics, and other such deep-water statistical analysis can shed light on valid conclusions, the reading audience for such published research would likely include only a fraction of hiring managers with backgrounds in industrial and organizational psychology or statistics.

Therefore, it appears that (1) the audience that could benefit the most from this research (hiring managers, human resources personnel) does not typically read the periodicals in which the research results are published, and (2) valid applicant attributes highlighted by such research are not the most highly valued by hiring managers. This research-application gap can be narrowed when both researchers and hiring managers/HR professionals communicate with each other in the language of the business case or the value proposition: How can these predictions be tracked to demonstrated results in the organization?

Job Interview Context: Social and Situational Influences on Hiring Decisions

After the cover letter and résumé review, the job interview is the second stop in the hiring process, which can be considered a staged release of information over time that attests to a candidate's expertise and value in the marketplace. To make it to the interview stage, the cover letter and the résumé must have first captured the interest of the hiring manager.

There are many variables in play before, during, and after the interview, not the least of which are the nonverbal and self-promotion behaviors of applicants. These behaviors, as well as the nature of the position to be filled, shape the nature of the interview and how hiring managers perceive the candidates. Because the impressions people make on others influence how others perceive, evaluate, and treat them, individuals often craft their behavior to create certain impressions in the minds of others. Hopefully, conveying the proper impression increases the chances that a candidate will achieve a preferred outcome, which may be a second interview, a job offer, a promotion, etc.

While the informal term *likeability* has been introduced here as a strategy to enhance the prospects of receiving a job offer, researchers refer to such behavioral tactics that indirectly influence hiring recommendations as *impression management*. Such an approach involves several cognitive methods all working simultaneously before, during, and after the interview:

- Candidate motivations for managing a type of impression (motivation increases as a function of the value or importance of the desired goal)
- Candidate approaches for creating a type of impression
- Hiring manager perceptions of how the candidate fits the corporate culture
- Hiring manager perceptions of candidate likeability (responding to impression management tactics by candidate)
- Hiring manager mood (which can influence degree of likeability)

Hiring manager perceptions of how a candidate meets the requirements for the open position involve a different context for assessing a candidate's qualifications — a context that will be addressed later.

All other things being equal, candidates are more motivated to manage their likeability factor for hiring managers who are powerful, of high status, or likeable. When the likeability factor runs in both directions, people connect at a level that more often than not makes it easier for a candidate to manage a particular impression.

If the idea of impression management sounds like it smacks of behavioral manipulation, you're right. In fact, public self-presentation is almost always overtly manipulative because the intent is to maximize projected benefits and minimize expected penalties. It's all about "putting your best foot forward" for nearly every social situation.

Self-presentation is an important component that defines where people fit in the social stratification, prepares the context and direction of interpersonal interactions, and manages "performance" for any and every behavior that is directed by a specific role, especially for a job. However, the extremes of impression management can result in behavior that is not conducive to fostering favorable impressions with hiring managers.

Finding the Right Balance of Impression Management

On the one end of the external impression-management[13] spectrum lie individuals who seem oblivious of other's reactions to their behaviors. While some may engage in conscious action to generate attention, these individuals often fail to process information in a manner that has any relevancy.

In other words, such people often direct their attention away from themselves to other persons, places, or things in their immediate

---

[13] *Internal impression management* is a term used to describe behaviors directed to the self as the primary audience (self-esteem, self-image), whereas *external impression management* describes behaviors directed to others as the primary audience.

environment, and therefore do not consider how others see their behavior. In essence, they have no feedback loop that allows them to adjust their behavior based on how others see them. During an interview, candidates with this impression-management style (fortunately, they are few and far between) do not find favor in the eyes of hiring managers.

At the other end of the impression-management spectrum are individuals with heightened public self-awareness, who note in a conscious manner every aspect of their appearance and behavior that is observed by others. Such people find it difficult *not* to focus on the impressions others are reaching about them. They purposely scan for visual, auditory, or body language cues, and respond selectively to cues that foster the "right" impression for a first date, job interview, audition, public speaking engagement, or any other particular situation.

In fact, this acute form of impression management can manifest itself as performance anxiety or stage fright for some actors, musicians, athletes — and interview candidates. Unfortunately, this impression-management style does not create a strong positive first impression with hiring managers.

Truth be told, most people monitor how others perceive them at a subconscious level without paying obvious attention. This subliminal self-monitoring can be attributed to many self-preservation behaviors that have become routine. Some candidates are motivated to carefully manage the impressions they project but refrain from doing so during interviews, perhaps based on the presence or absence of external cues, such as personal familiarity with the hiring manager or relationships with existing employees.

In general, the more expertise and accomplishments a candidate has, the more likely he or she will keep overt impression management at minimal levels, allowing expertise and achievement to speak for themselves. However, if a position is one for which there is significant competition, then an applicant will be more motivated to manage his or her impression in the hopes of obtaining some advantage.

The Language of Impression Management
The Cover Letter

The usual first instance of impression management occurs not during the interview but in the language of the cover letter. The vocabulary that fosters a positive impression with hiring managers focuses on two important considerations:

1. The needs and concerns of the hiring manager
2. Promotion of the *benefits* of the candidate's expertise going forward

The cover letter is not a summary of the résumé, yet that is exactly how the vast majority of candidates write their cover letters. Contrary to the advice of many career counselors and coaches, the cover letter should have a sales/marketing tone that speaks the language of the hiring manager with more instances of "you/your/yours" and far fewer instances of "I/me/my/mine." The purpose of the cover letter is to: (1) engage the busy hiring manager's interest with the first sentence (or within 5–7 seconds), (2) induce the hiring manager to read the entire cover letter, and (3) lead the hiring manager to review the résumé. The cover letter can be laced with assertive, *slightly* unabashed self-promotion language, as long as that language that both understands and supports the needs of the hiring manager.

The impression-management language in cover letters must have a tone that emphasizes the benefits of the candidate's expertise for the hiring manager going forward. By relating specific expertise to problems or issues facing the prospective hiring manager, the candidate creates a very strong impression as the candidate of choice for any position.

The chapter on cover letters goes into detail on incorporating the language of impression management.

The Résumé

A significant problem with candidate résumés is how so many ordinary task completions are passed off as "accomplishments." A task completion is part of a "duty and responsibility;" an accomplishment or achievement demonstrably contributes to the higher strategic objectives of the organization above and beyond daily duties and responsibilities. Task completions and duties and responsibilities highlight features of past experience, while achievements and accomplishments emphasize the benefits of a particular expertise.

The chapter on advanced résumé therapy provides details on integrating the language of impression management.

The Likeability Factor and Impression Management Are Forms of Persuasion You Should Master

The ability to captivate an audience, persuade others with opposing views, or influence the undecided is a gift few people naturally possess. However, the elements of the art of persuasion can be taught, learned, and applied. Behavioral scientists have demonstrated that persuasion is successful when it appeals to a restricted set of basic human drives and needs.

Dr. Robert Cialdini, author of *Influence: Science and Practice*, identified six fundamental principles of persuasion and how they can be applied in any organization (see Table 2). These principles underscore the premise that *creating the unique advantage is really about demonstrating that you serve the needs of others by being the best at solving their problems.*

Table 2. Six Fundamental Principles of Persuasion and Their Application (compiled from "Harnessing the Science of Persuasion," *HBR*, Oct. 2001. pp. 72–79)

Principle	Definition	Application
Liking	People like those who like them.	Uncover real similarities and offer genuine praise.
Reciprocity	People repay in kind.	Give what you want to receive.
Social Proof	People follow the lead of similar others.	Use peer power whenever it's available.
Consistency	People align with their clear commitments.	Make commitments active, public, and voluntary.
Authority	People defer to experts.	Expose your expertise; don't assume it is self-evident.
Scarcity	People want more of what they can have less of.	Highlight unique benefits and exclusive information.

The *likeability factor* is a critical component of impression management in many social interactions, but especially in the hiring process in today's competitive marketplace. Being aware of hiring manager prejudices and presuppositions, creating workable strategies for positive and influential self-presentation behaviors, and paying attention to the linguistic tactics that enhance impression presentation ("raising you likeability factor") will all place you in a favorable position with hiring managers as their candidate of choice.

FOUR: WHAT HIRING MANAGERS ARE LOOKING FOR IN CANDIDATES

Microsoft prioritizes intelligence for all jobs; Southwest Airlines hires first and foremost for attitude. In both companies, hiring managers look for people who can solve problems and provide solutions; they are not in the market for more employees. Unfortunately, most candidates in the workforce position themselves (through their cover letters, résumés, and interview strategies) in ways that fail to differentiate their expertise from other candidates; in other words, they present themselves as "just another potential employee."

According to a 2014 survey of human resource managers:[14]

- Companies continue to struggle to find skilled candidates…[because] candidates lacked the right technical abilities or work experience.
- Companies fail to choose the right talent for manager positions 82 percent of the time (Gallup, *Harvard Business Review*).
- Only 1 in 10 employees possess all the required traits to be a good manager because most were selected because of success in previous non-management roles, success in revenue-generating roles, or selected based on tenure.

---

[14] *HR Magazine*, Society of Human Resource Management, May 2014.

- Candidates lacked critical thinking/problem-solving skills, basic computer skills, English-language fluency, professionalism, and strong work ethic.
- Most preferred executive trait is the ability to motivate more than consistent high-level performance (also, strong ability to manage change, ability to identify and develop talent, and innovative thinking).

What Is "Talent" in the Job Market?

If the information in this section seems as though it is directed at hiring managers and not candidates, it was meant to apply to both audiences. Understanding the concepts behind what defines talent in today's job market helps both the hiring manager and candidate understand what the other expects.

According to a famous study by McKinsey & Company in 1998, talent can be defined as:

> ...*the sum of a person's abilities...his or her intrinsic gifts, skills, knowledge, experience, intelligence, judgment, attitude, character, and drive. It also includes his or her ability to learn and grow. [Talent refers to] the best and brightest...*[15]

However, since the recession of 2008, many organizations have begun placing less emphasis on "star" performers (the top 10–20 percent of the employee pool) because it reduces individual, team, and

---

[15] Chambers, E., Foulon, M., H. Handfield-Jones, S. Hankin, and E. Michaels III. "The war for talent," *The McKinsey Quarterly*, No. 3, 1998, pp. 44–57.

organizational performance. In addition, recent research[16] suggests the emergence of a new talent paradigm:

- General mental ability, not past performance, is the best predictor of future performance.
- IQ is the most powerful — but not only — predictor of job performance.
- Performance varies over time (in other words, today's "B team" player could be next year's "A team" player).
- People who believe intelligence is fixed learn less over time; people who believe intelligence is malleable continue getting smarter and more skilled at what they already can do and are more willing to learn new skills.
- Companies benefit more when they "grow" their star performers with training, mentoring, challenging projects, and public recognition.
- Companies that excel at talent management have a process with multiple owners, from the CEO, HR, and management at all levels.
- The "war for talent" and so-called "star wars" is a competitive context framing that promotes selective advancement (through forced rankings), resulting in overall lower productivity, inequity and skepticism, reduced collaboration, lower morale, and mistrust in leadership for all other employees.
- Just as a high tide lifts all boats, programs and opportunities for all employees to excel prove to be more effective than selective advancement.

---

[16] Pfeffer, J., and R. Sutton. *Hard Facts, Dangerous Half-Truths, and Total Nonsense: Profiting from Evidence-Based Management.* (Boston: Harvard Business School Press, 2006).

One important point to consider is that if only 10–20 percent of employees are rated as "star" talent, the other 80–90 percent of employees are performing the bulk of the necessary work. Organizations cannot afford to disregard the "B team" players because an organization's long-term performance depends more on the capabilities and contributions of the steady performers—the so-called "best supporting actors of the business world."[17] As Charles Dickens wrote in *A Tale of Two Cities*, "The needs of the many outweigh the needs of the few."

The *Knowing-Doing Gap* in Talent Management

Many companies and organizations are concerned about the *knowing-doing* gap in managing talent, whereby a functional separation exists between employee job knowledge and on-the-job performance. To close this knowing-doing gap, employers have implemented many creative solutions such as:

- Capitalizing on generational differences using *reverse mentoring*, whereby younger employees mentor older employees on new technology
- Traditional mentoring, where retirees are brought in to work on projects that allows them to share expertise with younger employees
- Employee career management through online resources and interactive assessments to fine-tune career development and direction

---

[17] DeLong, T. and V. Vijayaraghavan. "Let's hear it for B players," *Harvard Business Review*, June 2003, pp. 3–8.

- Corporations partnering with universities to create niche-focused degree programs in a variety of disciplines.

This knowing-doing gap is often evident in cover letters and résumés, where candidates place an emphasis on duties and responsibilities (knowing) rather than accomplishments and achievement (doing). *The best predictor of future performance is mental ability as demonstrated in a cover letter by highlighting the future benefits of expertise rather than the features of past performance.*

Figure 6. Talent Response Dimensions (from Beechler and Woodward, 2009)

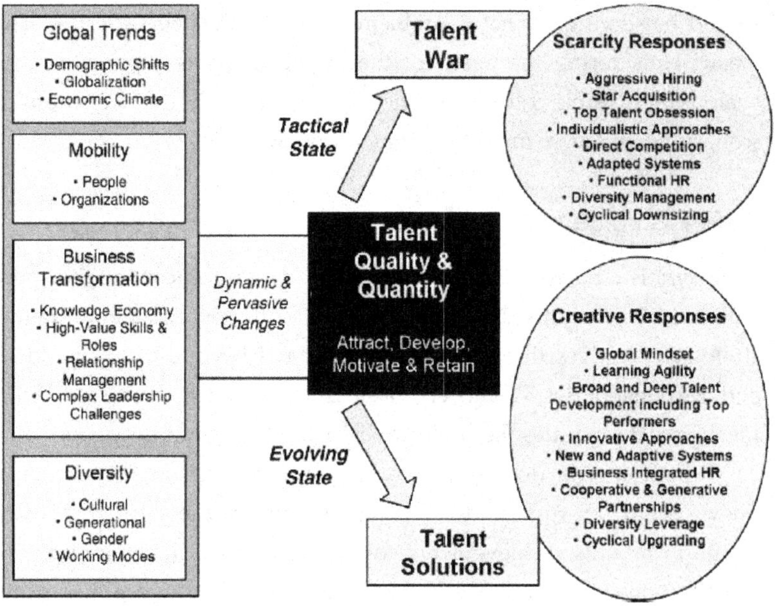

Schon Beechler and Ian Woodward. "The Global 'War for Talent'," *Journal of International Management* 15 (2009), pp. 273–285.

Guarding Against *Groupthink*

One other skill value-add candidates should possess is the ability to detect *groupthink* ("The Emperor's New Clothes" syndrome). Groupthink occurs when members of a group come to decisions that conform to the group's values and ethics. Groupthink is a defensive behavior that, while minimizing anxiety, unfortunately limits decision-making ability. Groupthink can also threaten decision integrity and organizational stability — the presence of an assertive or popular leader can sway decisions to favor a course of action that may not necessarily result in the best outcome. Candidates should keep in mind that they should be serving others as problem solvers with their expertise. This means considering the needs of the organization as a priority when evaluating possible courses of action. It's not unlikely that a groupthink scenario would arise in a situational interview.

Creating *Valueocity*

Valueocity is a term I coined about ten years ago to describe the speed with which an individual brings value to an organization's higher strategic objectives through efforts above and beyond ordinary duties and responsibilities. Valueocity is a differentiating factor for hiring managers; it separates the "employees" from the "game changers."

Which criteria do hiring managers use to find such candidates? They scour résumés for evidence of valueocity in listed accomplishments, achievements, recognized professional brand, and contributions to an organization's goals. When those accomplishments, achievements, and contributions can be quantified with costs avoided, revenues generated, and percentages improved, the candidate will attract the hiring manager's attention.

Where Candidates Fail

The vast majority of cover letters and résumés confuse the idea of a *task completion* with that of *accomplishment* or *achievement*. Bullet list items on a résumé that read "Generated reports for upper management" or "Led training for new employees" are sometimes listed under an "Accomplishments" heading when in fact they are task completions, which actually fall under the "duties and responsibilities" category. Good hiring managers know how to spot this failure to separate the two concepts.

An accomplishment or achievement demonstrably contributes to the higher strategic objectives of the organization beyond ordinary daily duties. Task completions, duties, and responsibilities are *features of your previous experience*; accomplishments and achievements are the *benefits of your expertise that have future application*.

Creating Functional Expertise from Tasks and Duties

Candidate résumés filled with bullet lists of tasks and duties/responsibilities don't go far enough to differentiate the applicant from others who may be equally qualified. Hiring managers want to see résumés that contain core competencies and functional expertise as shown in Figure 7.

Figure 7. What Hiring Managers Want to See on Résumés

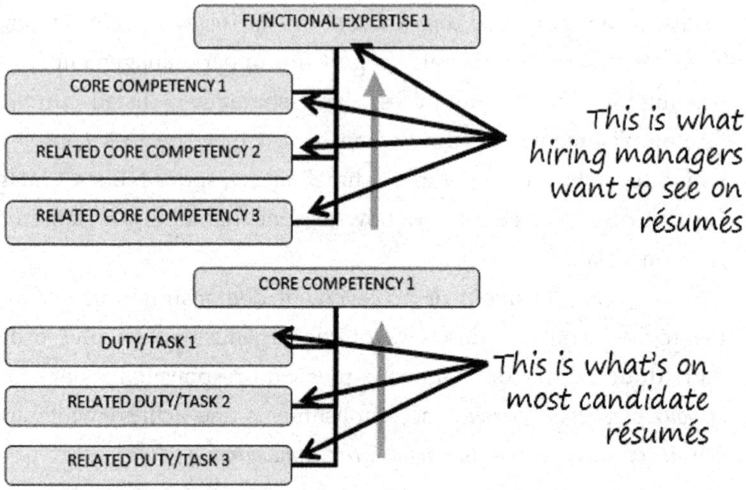

Core competencies, a combination of skill, knowledge, and expertise, fulfill three important criteria for hiring managers:

- Core competencies (unique or highly sought after skills, knowledge, experience) are difficult for a competitor to imitate.
- They can be repurposed for other products or markets (multiple application).
- They contribute to the end user's experienced benefits (they add value to products/services).

Several core competencies contribute to a functional expertise, which is simply a higher level of integrated skills, knowledge, and experience that work in concert with each other. A functional expertise also reflects a career-long exposure to a particular job or functional area as well as the problem-solving and challenges associated with that functional area.

It is *imperative* that, as a job candidate, you see the bigger picture of your expertise. Step outside of the job mentality and embrace how your core competencies help contribute toward an organization's *competitive advantage*. Visualize how your high-level functional expertise (technical, managerial, etc.) helps contribute toward an organization's *market dominance*. Figure 8 shows this relationship.

Figure 8. True Value of Core Competency and Functional Expertise

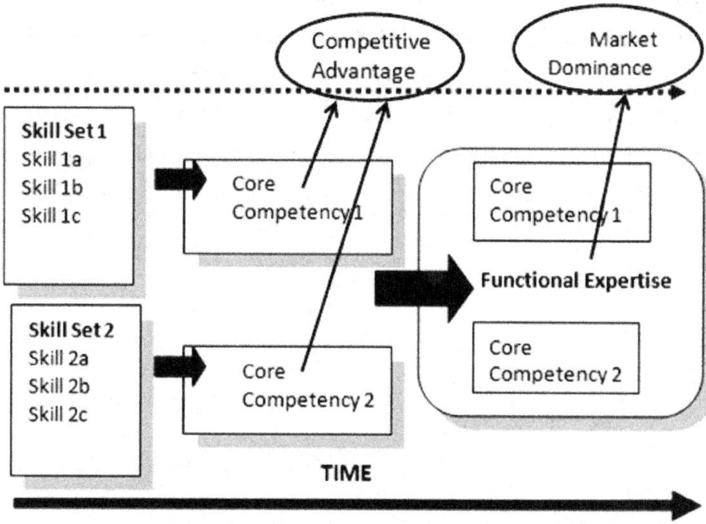

Hiring Manager and Candidate Common Ground

The following list showcases what hiring managers consider evidence of functional expertise.

- A résumé with accomplishments/achievements
- Articles published in peer-reviewed journals
- Profession-specific certifications and licenses
- Active participation in a professional association
- Presenting at regional/national conferences

- Teaching at conferences and/or local colleges
- Writing books/blog posts about the professional field
- Creating a professional LinkedIn profile that is updated often
- Serving as a resource for others in the profession

Job candidates should use this list as a guide in promoting their functional expertise.

One seminar attendee once opined that he (a consultant) and everyone else he knows doesn't have the time to do all of the things in the above list. Well, the idea is not to do them all at once but to develop a strategic plan that, over time, has you doing most or all of them. Start with the low-hanging fruit, such as creating a professional LinkedIn profile or an accomplishment-focused résumé and benefits-laden cover letter. Once those boxes have been checked, move on to the next most manageable task.

FIVE: THE CANDIDATE STRATEGY

Now we will explore effective candidate strategies for addressing the more subjective portion of hiring decisions.

Create a Professional Brand and Generate Positive Associations

The San Francisco Federal Reserve recently performed data analytics on Department of Labor data and discovered that *nearly 70 percent of Americans who land new jobs weren't even looking for one.* A 2013 study by the San Francisco Fed found that 42 percent of hires in any given month happen at companies that don't report vacancies. That's a very important reason for making sure that creating and promoting a professional brand should be part of your job or career search strategy.

Creating and promoting a professional brand helps candidates take advantage of unforeseen opportunities. Building corporate or product brand value involves two important components: (1) making others aware of the brand in question, and (2) creating a brand image that generates positive associations. The same principles apply in the workforce regardless of your specific employment arrangements. For individuals in permanent or contract employment positions, those wanting to move up the rungs of the internal corporate ladder, or those promoting their own business and seeking clients, the task is the same:

Create positive associations between quantified accomplishments and expertise, and the people with a need for that expertise. That way, others will promote that brand (building brand equity) based on a perceived professional and personal reputation in that specialty.

There are different opinions as to what factors contribute to a professional brand. I've found these three fundamental elements to be critical to creating a professional brand *and* solid reputation:

- Your **personal values** as revealed in your words and actions
- Your **ethics** as revealed in your words and actions
- Your **recognized expertise** (skills, knowledge, experience, and accomplishments) as listed on pages 63-64.

Also tied to these elements are the strengths of your expertise, the uniqueness of your professional or technical offering, and your likeability.

The Importance of Creating a Personal Connection

Candidates must present themselves based on the criteria of the position to which they are applying. Prior to any job interview, the hiring manager or human resources evaluates the hard requirements followed by evidence of preferred competencies as provided on the résumé. The cover letter should give some glimpse of the candidate's personality.

At the interview, those requirements and competencies receive top priority, but prior to and throughout the formal evaluation of the candidate's expertise, the hiring authority is assessing the candidate's personality. Personality — specifically, *likeability* — is the initial criteria evaluated because that first impression is set visually and then throughout the informal conversation that takes place before the formal interview.

Some career management consultants believe that the job market is dysfunctional because the likeability/personality dimension of hiring is rarely addressed as a requirement in job postings. They claim this omission in job postings places candidates at a disadvantage. I disagree. Who goes into a job interview — or *any* social interaction — not aware of this aspect of interpersonal communication?

The human factor plays a significant role in every hiring decision, whether or not the required interpersonal skills are highlighted in job postings. Any dysfunction, when it occurs, may lie with either the candidate *or* the hiring manager, each of whom might fail to understand the importance of personality and likeability as they influence both the first impression and the final hiring decision.

The subjective nature of the hiring process in today's job market *is what it is*, with each facet (objective assessments, intuitive reflection, subjective preference) providing the hiring manager a unique perspective on a candidate's potential for on-the-job success.

In the grand hiring scheme, improving flaws in a cover letter and résumé are relatively easy tasks compared to eliminating personality and behavioral issues that could impede a candidate's progress. A job interview is, after all, a social interaction, and the most salient behaviors exhibited by an applicant in such a situation are his or her social interaction skills.

Likeability is your first and last hurdle for any job or career pursuit. Likeability relates to friendliness, relevance, empathy, and "being real." Likeability works best when it's not forced or seen as an attempt to manipulate others. *Likeonomics* is simply a new term to describe the interpersonal and economic currency that connects people with other people, to new ideas, and to organizations where they share a variety of similar preferences. Likeability is connection driven. It's a new global currency that isn't made of paper or coin (or bitcoin) but whose denominations come in different types of relationships.

The *Journal of Occupational and Organizational Psychology* states that favorable first impressions created by candidates during the rapport-building stage of job interviews (that is, small talk) influenced interviewers' subsequent evaluations. This conclusion confirms other research that found that the most valid candidate attributes (skills, knowledge, experience) are not always those the hiring manager values most when making a decision to hire.

All expertise being equal among candidates, most hiring managers hire the candidate who makes a memorable impression on a personal and professional level throughout the entire hiring process, but especially in the beginning. In other words, if you present yourself as a likeable person during the interview, hiring managers tend to be more interested in what you have to offer in the way of skills, knowledge, experience, and accomplishments. A positive first impression automatically opens the *door of receptivity*, so that the hiring manager may eventually think: "This person can help the team, the business unit, and the company achieve its goals — and I like him/her."

However, if you don't connect on a personal level or there is any perceived personality threat to an otherwise well-oiled team, you may not receive a job offer. In life and business, it's not what or who you know — *it's who you know that likes you.*

I have observed over the course of my career that the people who excel in their careers understand two key secrets to their likeability: (1) fostering relationships with peers, subordinates, and upper management; and (2) clearly communicating with those same individuals.

Make no mistake, your ability to manage relationships will pay huge dividends as others embrace and even promote your professional brand in the workplace. A *dislikeability factor*, on the other hand, will leave you with a feeling of constantly having to swim upstream in the workplace.

True Story: Branding Gone Wrong + Groupthink + Poor Relationship Management = Major Fail

I once got into an email discussion with an engineering director a couple of pay grade levels above me about a concern I had with the engineering department's decision to use interchangeable brand names for two different types of microprocessors. He challenged my assertion that commingling the brand names would confuse customers; he was of the opinion that it didn't matter. My team and I were putting the finishing touches on the complex microprocessor documentation for one of the microprocessor families, and I argued that we needed to resolve this branding issue before finalizing the many documents and thousands of pages of information.

When he pushed, I pushed right back. I cited relevant research and outlined how it would be a huge—and costly— marketing mistake to feed the new and different product line into the existing established one. Throughout this back-and-forth email debate, we copied all the marketing directors; not one of them joined in the discussion. The silence was, in fact, deafening. Because the CEO and president (that is, the two owners) were engineers with PhDs and were known to fire executives on the spot for voicing dissenting opinions, the marketing directors stayed mum. Better to stay quiet and "save face" than confront the great and powerful Oz. This was groupthink placed on mute.

Thus, my position that Brand XYZ was not an extension of Brand ABC fell on deaf ears. And despite my cogent and relevant arguments, the engineering director refused to take my viewpoint into consideration.

Long story short, the product line was merged with Brand ABC, because it was much easier for the engineering director to keep his job at the executive level by agreeing with a wrong decision than to advocate for an unpopular decision—a classic characteristic of groupthink. Shortly thereafter, the engineering director resigned to "pursue other career opportunities." In the high-tech world, that's usually a euphemism for getting fired or being asked to resign.

Did our disagreement have anything to do with it? I don't know, but it had me thinking about this individual's knowledge of creating brand identity and brand equity (in fact, why was an engineering director controlling branding discussions when it was really *marketing's* job?). Why was he pushing back on what I thought were sensible, research-backed ideas?

From what I later learned, this engineering director lacked certain relationship-building skills with others higher up on the corporate ladder. Yes, he stepped outside of his domain expertise (engineering) by insisting the two brands be combined and that there would be no downstream (i.e., customer) issues – even when presented with a rational, logical argument for keeping the brands separated and understanding how the brand equity is determined. His disregard for wise council from others – and how he responded to suggestions – ultimately led to his exiting the company.

There's a lesson to be learned here. You may possess all the technical or professional skills necessary to perform your job at a high level, but what really propels you upward and forward in your career are your verbal and written communications skills – including your ability to evaluate your own self-talk, to know your domain of expertise, and to know when you're out of your league. You also need to nurture relationships up AND down the organization ladder.

Getting into Their Heads: Associative Models

Personal brand identity and brand equity are 21st century terms for personal reputation and reputation value, respectively. The process that connects other people with your personal brand and even helps enhance your brand value starts in the brain. Our memory consists of nodes of stored information connected by neural links of varying strength. When a node is activated by external information or by retrieval from long-term memory, it stimulates other memory nodes. When the activation of another memory node exceeds some threshold, information in that node is recalled.

For example, when considering a fast-food purchase, you might think of McDonald's because of its strong association with that product category. Your knowledge associated with McDonald's comes to mind — such as the Golden Arches, or the Happy Meal packaging (what parent doesn't want their kids to be happy?), or the taste of their French fries. Or maybe you recall images from a TV commercial with Ronald McDonald or simply past experiences with the franchise.

This process is termed *associative network memory model*[18] and, consistent with this model, brand knowledge is conceived as consisting of a brand node in memory in which many associations are linked. See Figure 9 for a simple illustration of this associative network memory model.

Figure 9. Graphic Representation of Associative Network Memory Model

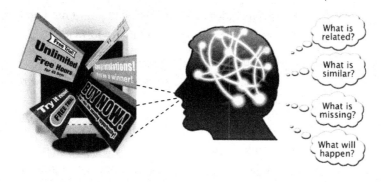

---

[18] Anderson, John R. *The Architecture of Cognition*. (Cambridge: Harvard University Press, 1982).

71

Here are several specific ways to become embedded in the *associative models* of hiring managers and others with a need for your expertise:

- Write articles for peer-reviewed journals in your professional field.

- Give presentations or workshops at meetings and conferences and with other associations in your professional specialty or field.

- Network with other professionals in your specific field.

- Use social media (blogs, YouTube, Twitter, LinkedIn, etc.) to expand your circles of influence. (However, be sure you have something valuable to say; the virtual world is already overflowing with mindless blather.)

- Write a book on issues facing your profession or field.

- Create your own attention-grabbing blog name and catchphrase.

- Create a unique sign-off statement for each blog entry with your brand statement.

- Write a bio that includes more details about your brand and its unique edge rather than the typical obituary format.

The more unique your niche, the stronger your brand can become. A positive brand image works in three significant ways to help create an unique advantage:

- It helps solidify your position in any internal or external job or career opportunity.

- It can differentiate your expertise from your competition and move it toward "preferred candidate" status.

- It can command a higher salary and encourage hiring managers to seek you out.

What you need to deliver:

- A **professional brand** that promotes your expertise directed at the hiring manager's needs and interests as a forward-looking strategy ("what I can do for you moving forward" versus "what I have done for others in the past")
- A **professional portfolio** of documentation that attests to your expertise
- A **plan for promoting your expertise** throughout the entire hiring cycle

Promoting Your Professional Brand in the Marketplace

Promoting your professional brand requires the same approach whether your interest is in pursuing a permanent position (internal or external), seeking contracting opportunities, or expanding a consulting business. The common denominator of this approach is assuming an attitude of being in business for yourself and promoting your accomplishments (quantified, if possible) as solutions to the problems of others.

It is more difficult to build and promote a professional brand with only "duties and responsibilities" on a résumé because *everyone* with a job has them. Duties, responsibilities, and task completions provide little in the way differentiating you from other candidates. Truly successful individuals understand that, no matter where the paycheck comes from, they really do work for themselves. Contractors and consultants know what being self-employed is all about. Sometimes people in hourly or salaried positions lose sight of the fact that they are, in a sense, "self-employed" as well. Employers don't keep employees on the payroll out of the goodness of their hearts; they issue paychecks on a regular basis as a reward for the daily application of both hard and soft skills.

Protecting Your Professional Brand

It seems that every week there's another story about someone sabotaging his or her career with a variety of social media tools like Facebook, Twitter, Instagram, SnapChat, or YouTube. Do people not stop to think about the ramifications of their rants and antics when the very people they mock become witnesses to their stupidity? Why are people in such a rush to ruin their reputations?

A 2012 survey of 5,000 people by Microsoft discovered that 56 percent of adults don't actively think about consequences of online activities; 14 percent of adults have experienced negative consequences due to online activities by others (21 percent were fired from a job; 16 percent lost out on getting a job; 16 percent lost their health insurance; 14 percent lost out on the college of their choice; and 15 percent were turned down for a mortgage).

Whether it's government bureaucrats partying on the taxpayers' dime and posting photos and music videos of their hijinks, or high-profile politicians posting lewd photos of themselves online, the complete absence of forethought for the ramifications of such behavior has long-term consequences, both on and off the Internet. People get disciplined or even fired for such imbecilic behavior, but their lapses of discernment linger for far longer in cyberspace.

Has common sense taken a holiday? Has the world's doofus population exploded? Inquiring minds, not the least of which are those of hiring managers, want to know.

Such behavior is nothing new—it's always been around—it's just that now people have the opportunity to instantly broadcast their antics to the entire world through various social media outlets.

When creating and promoting your professional brand for the job market or a career move, navigating the social media landscape can be like walking across a minefield. If you want to protect your professional brand, you have to be selective—not only with which applications you choose to use, but with what you choose to reveal to the world.

Your brand consists of three fundamental components: your specialized professional or technical expertise; your public image or persona; and your personal values. People whose professional brand is centered on strong personal values—who possess a rock-solid moral, ethical compass—rarely allow themselves to fall into compromising situations. They understand that their professional brand is more than just what they excel at doing; it's who they excel at *being* that is the higher value.

Watch Your *&^%@# Language!

If you've ever wondered about people who stream profanity at work like they were real-life *South Park* characters, well, it's official (as if we needed a study to confirm it): According to a CareerBuilder survey of 2,000 hiring managers and 3,800 U.S. workers, 64 percent of employers said that they'd think less of an employee who repeatedly uses profanity and 57 percent would be less likely to promote that person.

The study also revealed that 51 percent of workers surveyed admitted to using profane language in the office (understandable if you work with computers using a certain operating system), and 95 percent of those folks said they do so in front of coworkers while 51 percent admitted to using foul language in conversations with their managers. But, angels that we all are, we are less likely to use expletives in front of senior management and clients.

Employers found that employees who possess and display a profanity-laced vocabulary appear less professional, seem to have self-control and maturity issues, and 50 percent thought that such language made an employee appear less intelligent.

The study revealed that profanity is most often heard when levels of stress or tension are elevated, but then again there are some people who use such language *regardless* of stress, frustration, or tension. Just watch any reality TV show and count the number of bleeps heard. Why would anyone think that using such language in front of TV cameras *enhances* the perception viewers have of them?

The CareerBuilder survey found that Washington, DC, was the worst when it came to swearing at work (I don't think "swearing in" counted here), and Philadelphia was the "least worst" in the Top 10 job markets in the U.S. As for age groups, the worst was the 35–44 age group (sure, they have kids, college educations, and mortgages to pay for); the "least worst" was the 18–24 age group, with the over–55 age group right behind.

From a job and career perspective, your use of vocabulary on the job influences the perceptions others have of you. Profanity in the office does negatively impact that perception and could be a limiting factor for your career success.

Two anonymous individuals penned great quotes about the use of profanity:

"Profanity is the weapon of the witless."
"When a man uses profanity to support an argument, it indicates that either the man or the argument is weak – probably both."

Moving Beyond the Professional Brand: Building Your Platform

A platform is a raised area of flooring. That's an apt description for another type of "platform" which elevates someone with expert-level skills and knowledge above the crowd of also-rans. Your *platform* is a level of professional accomplishment that extends your highly sought-after professional brand.

Your platform, very simply, is the expertise you have developed that gives you visibility, authority, and a proven influence within a targeted population, such as a particular profession, market, or field.

That expertise is distributed through a website, social media presence, publications, seminars, speeches, workshops, and so on.

Platform building is most often associated with how people with specific expertise and knowledge promote that expertise and knowledge to others with a need for it. Book authors are one group that immediately comes to mind. They create different channels for how their information is disseminated through readings, book signings, social media, speeches, media contacts, workshops, and so on for the purpose of creating value for others and themselves. It is not about getting one million "likes" on Facebook or adding more Twitter followers. It is about building quality relationships over time.

In a similar fashion, job candidates should "distribute" their expertise in as many different avenues as their target audience frequents. They should create connections with potential hiring managers or new clients by dispensing their expertise in traditional formats and social media those individuals likely frequent.

Let's look at four major areas of platform building for extending your expertise:

- **Niche Visibility**: Who knows you? Who knows your work or accomplishments? How do you communicate to others outside of your immediate job? What is it you do or have done? How many people are aware of it? How does your visibility get "distributed"? What communities (online, professional associations, etc.) are you a member of? Basically, where do you make waves and how often do you make them?

- **Niche Authority**: How solid is your credibility? Are you published in your field? What are your credentials? (It's not about how many degrees, licenses, or certifications you have, but whether you have the right ones for the right field of work).

- **Proven Influence**: Don't claim to be an influencer, because anyone can toss about such pseudo-marketing terms. Show where your work has made an impact and provide demonstrable proof of that impact (quantitative measures such as costs avoided, revenues generated, and percentages improved really help). Avoid the term *thought leader*, as it's such a cliché in marketing where there's no way to demonstrate how many thoughts you've led (to who knows where).

- **Target Population**: Are you most visible to the most appropriate target audience? In other words, is your work helping build your brand within the circles where you already have visibility? What about related peripheral areas? Can you extend your expertise into these area?

Building your platform is all about putting in a consistent effort from one year to the next—not by calling attention to yourself, but by extending your network of people who are drawn to your brand. It's building the platform to a point when it starts speaking for who you are (personal values), what you do (reputation), and how you do it (expertise).

Platform building is the next level of extending your professional brand, and it is an organic process that evolves over time and circumstances.

The New Way to Network

Closely related to platform building is understanding how to properly network with other professionals who can help promote your brand equity. Networking is so often thought of as a technique for finding a job. While that is true, many people fail to grasp the fundamentals. There are new rules to networking today, rules that focus on a smaller, but more focused network of contacts, rules that emphasize mutually beneficial exchanges of information and opportunities. Old-school networking, where the expectation was for the many to help the one, is passé, having been replaced with a more results-oriented way of everyone reaping the benefits of a newly designed and balanced cooperativeness.

Here are some fundamentals of the New Networking:

- **Limit the size of your business or career network to 20 or fewer people**. Anything larger than that and it becomes too large to manage, particularly when the New Networking is based on reciprocal relationships with those who share similar goals or values.

- **Use the *80/20 Rule* with people in your network**. Over time, you'll discover your network assumes a natural stratification of individuals, separated by the degree of influence they have with others, or perhaps by some special knowledge or information in which you both share an interest. Using the 80/20 Rule, you'll devote 80 percent of your time and effort cultivating the relationships with those 20 percent of individuals where the cooperative gain is optimized.

- **Be an initiator of introductions**. Don't wait for others to ask "who do you know who…". Be proactive; initiate the process yourself. Put people together with common or complementary interests and you'll find that others are more inclined to do the same for you. Think of individuals in your network who would benefit from forming relationships with each other.

- **Collaborative networking means sharing knowledge**. I once worked in an engineering organization where the lead engineer hoarded critical information until the last minute and then let loose the "diving catch" to the amazement of upper management. The problem was solved, the customer was happy, and it all looked like one person's effort. At nearly every quarterly employee meeting, he received one of the "Special Achievement" awards for his work—until he got laid off, to the surprise of no one in his engineering organization. Because of his information stockpiling tendencies, he alienated his team members, thereby negating any possibility of them being members of his job-search network. What goes around…

Over my career, I discovered that the people who get great job offers or accelerate upward in the organization are the ones who act as information expediters and who are always willing to share their knowledge, skill, or expertise.

None of this is rocket science, nor is it "secrets unleashed" about networking. It's a common sense way of serving others before serving yourself. In fact, it more resembles how your grandmother served Thanksgiving meals—ensuring all others were fed first before sitting down and partaking of the meal herself. By doing so, she got what she wanted: the family together, everyone sharing a meal together, everyone else clearing the table, washing the dishes, pots, and pans, and storing the leftovers in Tupperware containers.

- **Maintain a 50/50 balance with the 80/20 Rule.** This fundamental gets back to the idea of a "balanced cooperativeness." While you don't have to keep score with the 20 percent in your network, you want to always keep in mind how mutual your network relationships truly are, because that's the only way the New Networking is successful. Once things are out of balance (you are giving more than you are receiving, or you are taking more than you are giving), it's time to honestly reassess that relationship and how it's being nurtured.

Here are what author and platform builder extraordinaire Christina Katz calls the "golden rules for platform builders" in her book, *Get Known Before the Book Deal*:[20]

- Be self-aware, not self-absorbed.
- Be intentional, not driven.
- Be responsive, unless you have chosen to be less available for a period of time.
- Keep an even keel, even in the face of upsets.
- Maintain a relaxed focus, but don't get sloppy.
- Acknowledge your humanity; you will surely make mistakes.
- Play nicely with others; have boundaries with those who can't or won't.
- Be golden like the rules; stay clear and on track.

What Is Your *Value Proposition*?

Any perceived value others have of you — especially if you are a new employee or are new to a team — is converted to actual value when you can clearly articulate how you have and can deliver bottom-line results. Your "favorable first impression" index is at the top of the scale when you don't have to fumble for a response to questions about your expertise.

What is a *value proposition*? It is simply a promise of value to be delivered to a targeted audience that clearly states:

- How your expertise solves problems or better positions your audience (hiring manager, contract manager, client, etc.)

---

[20] Katz, Christina. *Get Known Before the Book Deal*, (Cincinnati: Writer's Digest Books, 2008), p. 88.

81

- How your audience benefits from your expertise (quantified value)
- Your unique differentiation (why you are the best available solution or what's different from/better than what other candidates may offer)
- The benefits of your expertise in the language of your target audience (which may be different from how *you* speak to your skills, knowledge, and experience)

Your value proposition can be a headline and subheading or a short paragraph with a unique visual, such as a logo or headshot photo that can be read and understood in five seconds. The headline is the ultimate benefit: one sentence or phrase followed by a brief descriptive subheading or tagline. Support that tagline with three bulleted benefits. Don't underestimate the communicative power of a well-designed graphic or photo to reinforce your compelling proposition. Keep in mind that your value proposition doesn't have to be unique to be effective, but it must have "stickiness" to latch on to those associative models in the minds of your target audience.

A professional value proposition is the core of any career strategy and is a message that describes how you as an individual uniquely create value for clients, companies, and stakeholders. It is the primary reason why your services should be selected by a prospective employer or client over all other competitors. It is an elevator pitch of sorts that answers the question: "Why should I hire *you*?" The elements that comprise your professional brand support the essential message of your professional value proposition. The two, bundled together, remove all others from consideration for the job or contract.

Be Aware of Your Blind Spots

We all have blind spots in our personal makeup. Sometimes we need feedback from others to bring them to our awareness. Blind spots result from poor self-awareness and self-knowledge, and might manifest as saying one thing and doing another. Blind spots can be a career liability when the mistakes we make and the shortcomings we possess fail to produce a change in our awareness or knowledge of them.

Peak performers are not without their deficiencies; however, peak performers are aware of them, can improve on them, or can partner with others who possess the competency they lack.

Always be willing to admit mistakes or shortcomings. "Saving face" always backfires, as does having others assume an "Emperor's New Clothes" attitude, colluding with your denial. It's never a good idea to obscure the truth; that only prevents real gains in productivity or effectiveness.

Here are some major blind spots that anyone on any rung on the corporate ladder can possess: [21]

- **Runaway ambition**: winning at any cost, exaggerates accomplishments, arrogant
- **Unrealistic goals**: sets overly ambitious, unattainable goals for group; unrealistic about effort required
- **Relentless striving**: compulsive overachiever who sacrifices everything else, vulnerable to burnout
- **Drives others**: catalyst for burnout of others, prefers to micromanage rather than delegate, abrasive, insensitive

---

[21] From a study of 42 executives by Robert E. Kaplan; also referenced in Daniel Goleman's book, *Emotional Intelligence*.

- **Power hungry**: seeks power for self-interest rather than organization's; exploits others for personal gain
- **Recognition hound**: addicted to glory, takes credit for others' success, short on follow-through
- **Preoccupation with appearances**: style over substance, concerned more with image than results, craves prestige
- **Need to appear perfect**: visibly angered by criticism, blames others for failure, can't admit mistakes/weakness

When your self-awareness and self-knowledge are healthy, blind spots are more often than not behaviors or patterns you'll recognize yourself. However, that doesn't mean you shouldn't seek honest feedback on how others perceive you and your actions.

Understand the Factors That Influence Your Promotability

Your promotability within the organization hinges on several key variables: (1) your effectiveness as a problem solver; (2) the consistent quality of your work; (3) your communication skills; (4) your attitude on the job—and about the job; and (5) how you promote yourself in the work environment.

- **Your Effectiveness as a Problem Solver.** This should go without saying: Your promotability quotient gets higher as your effectiveness as a problem solver increases. Your performance shows your ability to deliver solutions. Problem solvers help generate revenue, avoid costs, improve efficiencies, and otherwise contribute to the higher strategic objectives of the organization.
- **Your Consistent Quality of Work.** This aspect of promotability involves taking ownership of projects and acting with a sense of urgency, striving to complete them ahead of schedule and under budget.

- **Your Communication Skills.** You'll find over the course of
  your working life that, as you ascend in the organization (or
  across organizations with job changes), your communication
  style must evolve with each new position of increased
  responsibility. As a team member, your communication skills
  are direct and immediately relevant to others. When you
  manage the team, your communication skills must be
  sharpened because of the nature of the messages you convey to
  subordinates.

As your career develops, your communication skills become more
refined because your messages change from people and project issues
to establishing direction, forging a mission, and ultimately, to setting a
vision. The communication skills of the first-line manager are different
from those of the corporate vice-president or CEO because of the
content of the messages.

- **Your Attitude on the Job — and About the Job.** I've seen
  highly capable technical people with lousy attitudes get passed
  over for promotion in favor of less capable individuals who
  possessed a very positive attitude. Much as an ill-fitting suit
  says something about the wearer, a bad attitude says
  something about the individual. A bad attitude affects an
  employee's approach to the job, work quality, interactions with
  others, and self-image — and it does not invite promotability.

- **How You Promote Yourself in the Work Environment.** The
  best time to influence your promotability is well before an
  opportunity opens up for promotion. Build your network of
  influencers before you need their help; this will remove the
  perception that you are just jockeying for position for the
  promotion. Ideally, you want others to think of you first when
  an opportunity opens up.

Master Your Emotional Competencies to Solidify Your Brand

Many of the best performers and achievers I have had the privilege of working with or managing excelled in more than one *soft-skill competency*. Soft-skill competencies are critical components of a strong, comprehensive professional brand.

I'm not speaking about technical skills, because a brilliant Linux software programmer who also has great organizational skills may completely lack social graces when dealing directly with people. There are lots of such folks in the workplace. They mistakenly believe that core competencies can be developed in isolation, without the need for building relationships with others. It's that missing element that often prevents these individuals from building a more rewarding and successful career. They may say they are happy working in isolation away from others, but for many it's more of a coping mechanism than a personal preference.

The individuals I'm referring to are those who can synergize the emotional intelligence competencies of motivation, self-regulation, self-awareness, empathy, and social skills to reach a critical mass of peak performance that energizes brand equity.

In a study of IBM and PepsiCo executives,[22] researchers discovered that, of those who scored strongest in six to seven core competencies, 87 percent were in the top one-third as reflected in their bonuses for their performance of the divisions they led. Those who scored lowest in those same competencies had outstanding performances only 13–20 percent of the time (as measured across offices around the world).

The emotional competencies that most often pointed to this high degree of performance and success were:

---

[22] Hay/McBer study of IBM and PepsiCo study as cited by Daniel Goleman in *Working with Emotional Intelligence*. Highly recommended read.

- Initiative, achievement, drive, and adaptability
- Influence, team leadership, and political awareness
- Empathy, self-confidence, and developing others

It is interesting that, of the ten items on this list, five reflect an awareness of and sensitivity to others: influence, team leadership, political awareness, empathy, and developing others. When these executives were firing on all cylinders, they were using their emotional competencies and as a result they — and their organizations — performed at their peak levels.

In *Working with Emotional Intelligence,* author Daniel Goleman writes that sales agents for a large cosmetic firm who were selected for their emotional competence had 63 percent less turnover during their first year than those whose selection disregarded their competence profile.

Everyone owns these emotional competencies; the only difference is the degree to which they are integrated into a professional brand.

SIX: THE ROLE OF PROFESSIONAL CREDENTIALS IN THE JOB MARKET

Not all professional credentials are created equal. They're vital for professionals seeking to advance or change careers, but the extent of credential value and use varies from one industry to the next. Therefore, it's important to understand exactly how a professional credential or designation can best serve your career aspirations.

Many credentials are awarded after rigorous exams and verified experience; some may require degree standing as well. They attest to the knowledge and expertise of the credential holder. The proper credentials can make it easier to climb the corporate ladder with your current employer or help push doors open a little wider in those professions on the periphery of your functional expertise.

Core Competencies

When I worked as a geologist/geophysicist with Phillips Petroleum from 1980 to 1985, one of my unofficial responsibilities was to serve as the division's editor for all technical papers that we sent to journals or conferences. I was also part of the first group of geologists to become certified on Intergraph digital workstations that were used for oil and gas exploration mapping.

That weeklong class paid off when I got laid off from my last oil company job in 1986. Nine months later, I got a job as a technical writer/editor for a company that developed geological mapping software—for use on Intergraph digital workstations and other large computers. You can see the relationship between the two careers that the certification helped bridge. My résumé at the time (using the functional format) focused more on my technical and computer skills than my geology/geophysics skills and experience because those were the skills that had the best chance of being transferred to a tangential field.

And that is the key to using credentials, certifications, or licenses when changing careers. Too often I encounter people who fail to appreciate how certifications are used for career enhancement. They think that a particular certification in the new career field is all they need for a job. It just doesn't work that way.

Imagine that your functional expertise is a large circle (see Figure 10), and all the ancillary skills, knowledge, and expertise (called *core competencies*) are smaller circles overlapping all around the edge of the larger circle. Some circles have a larger overlap than others, depending on the strength of the expertise in those peripheral areas. Career changes are easiest to manage when the transition is from an *existing* functional expertise to one of the *overlapping* core competencies (Numbers 3 and 4 in Figure 10). In time, that core competency becomes the *new* functional expertise.

Figure 10. Functional Expertise with Surrounding Core Competencies

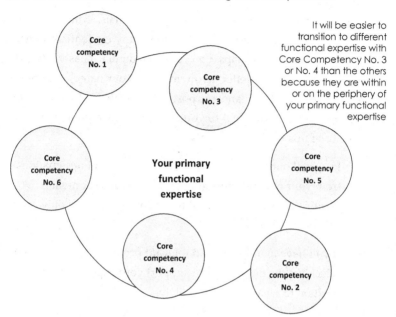

Career changes are far more difficult when trying to move from one functional expertise to another—jumping from one large circle to another with very little or no overlap. Usually, such career changes involve additional education (college degrees, other certifications and licenses, etc.) not to mention some experience in that field. Be mindful that many recent college graduates (RCGs—they get their own acronym) are entering the workforce already armed with cutting-edge knowledge and the latest skills. With mid-career changers and college graduates competing for the same positions, the lower compensation requirements for RCGs in many instances decide who will get hired.

When Credentials Attack

There is such a thing as having too many credentials. While the proper mix can enhance your career potential, too many credentials signal to hiring managers that perhaps you're a "credential chaser" (seeking even more three- or four-letter acronyms after your name) who prefers image over the substance and purpose of credentials. Too much of a good thing can be detrimental to your job and career strategy. So, here are some brief tips to help avoid this trap:

- Purge all outdated, irrelevant certifications and designations from your résumé and signature block. Those non-valid certifications scream, "My skills are outdated and I only rarely update my résumé."

- If you have many valid and relevant professional designations, select just the ones that best support your expertise for the position to which you are applying.

- Hiring managers are interested in only those certifications and licenses you actually possess. Do not list the courses you took along the way or what you hope to complete in the near future. In some instances, candidates use this approach to disguise the fact that they do not have the requisite educational requirements. Hiring managers are wise to this ploy.

- If you work in the public sector and have a long list of certifications or designations obtained through government training and testing, keep them in a separate document that can be used as part of your documentation portfolio. Place just those certifications that are relevant to the position on your résumé.

The proper professional credentials demonstrate to others a specialized expertise earned through testing and experience.

Professional designations enhance your personal brand, help build your brand equity, and add to the elements of your unique advantage.

SEVEN: SELLING THE FUTURE BENEFITS OF YOUR EXPERTISE IN COVER LETTERS

"Talk in terms of the other person's interests."
— Dale Carnegie
How to Win Friends and Influence People

Every so often someone asks me, "Do I really need a cover letter these days, even when a job ad doesn't ask for one?" Some hiring managers think that cover letters are a waste of time and say they don't read them. Well, they often don't read them because job seekers write them as an afterthought instead of developing them with purpose. It's a fact that the majority of cover letters fail in their attempt to immediately interest the hiring manager to read further.

However, if you write your cover letter correctly, it will be another document in your portfolio that attests to your professional expertise and your brand. It summarizes at a high level — with a touch of marketing panache — the accomplishments and capabilities detailed on your résumé with only *minimal* repetition.

You'll write your best cover letters after you've polished your résumé, in much the way a book author writes the preface after finishing the manuscript. Your cover letter, containing *some* raw materials from your résumé, will then propel hiring managers back to your résumé.

Hiring managers who don't read cover letters and proceed directly to the résumés often miss out on candidates who might be a notch above the competition simply because of how they're selling their professional brand. These hiring managers might inadvertently pass over the problem solver, the solutions provider, and the game changer, all whom their teams or companies need.

Use Direct Mail Strategies to Create an Effective Cover Letter

The cover letter is another form of documentation that attests to your professional brand. In my seminars and personal consultations, I always emphasize how the best cover letters include elements of great advertising copywriting. A well-written direct mail piece emphasizes product or service benefits to the customer; a well-written cover letter emphasizes the benefits of your expertise to the hiring manager. A well-written direct mail piece retains control of the next step by asking for the sale in the closing paragraph; a well-written cover letter takes control of the next contact by telling the hiring manager to expect a follow-up phone call to continue the dialogue about how the candidate's expertise is just what the hiring manager has been looking for.

The cover letter should have a tone that says: *I understand your business and the issues you face every day. You have found that value-add professional who has a demonstrated record of accomplishment and success and who can do the same for your company.*

Here is a cover letter strategy based on good direct mail techniques:

1. **Create a flowchart describing your expertise (skills, knowledge, experience and most importantly, your achievements) and why that expertise is necessary.** Before you write a single word on your cover letter, it is vital to establish in your own mind what your specialty is—what your professional brand offers and why the hiring manager cannot live without it. This may sound simple on the surface, but this step requires deep thought and consideration. Really think

about what you have to offer and the benefits that the hiring manager will reap by hiring you. Write down all of these points and refer to this list as you draft your cover letter. The flowchart should cover the following: the *needs* of the hiring manager, the *solution* you provide, and the *benefits* to the hiring manager.

2. **Establish the need and a link to the hiring manager.** Do this in the first sentence and paragraph of your letter. You know the challenges and issues facing the hiring manager and the particular profession or industry. Use this paragraph to drive home two points: (1) that you and the hiring manager have something in common, and (2) that your expertise is the solution he or she needs.

3. **Offer the hiring manager a solution.** Now that you have established that link between you and the hiring manager and mentioned the challenges, you need to provide him or her with a solution. This section of your cover letter should inform the hiring manager that your expertise is the answer to their problem. You have the expertise that he or she has been looking for, supported with proven past accomplishments (not duties or responsibilities) pertinent to the position. This section should be written in a positive and enthusiastic tone (see the examples at the end of this chapter).

4. **Drive home the benefits that the hiring manager will reap from your expertise.** You've gotten the hiring manager to this point—he knows he needs what you have to offer, and he knows you're going to help him in some way. Now, he needs to know the benefits of your expertise if he hires you. Direct mail copywriting understands that purchases are often made

based not on logic, but rather emotion—much the way hiring decisions are made.

5. **Consider providing a special offer.** You've laid the groundwork for your pitch; now it's time to drive home the point that you are the problem-solving expert for which the hiring manager has been looking. This suggestion may only be for the brave, but consider offering the hiring manager an enticement that will get him to take some action, such as a "try me before you hire me" option.

    -   Offer to work for free for a week as a "tryout" for the position. The job market is always highly competitive regardless of the state of the economy, and you need to be able to offer the hiring manager something that will get him to seriously consider hiring you.
    -   The "try me before you hire me" approach may be just the trick. Even if a hiring manager doesn't take you up on that offer (most won't for various policy or legal reasons), the fact that you are willing to work for free for a week sends a strong message about your confidence and your ability to hit the ground running. If it works, it's a way to instantaneously eliminate the competition for the position—as long as you deliver during that week.

6. **Reinforce your message and control the next contact.** Use the last paragraph to reinforce the entire cover letter. Remind the hiring manager why she needs your expertise, what it will do for her, and how that value-add will contribute to the company's success. Always initiate the next contact in your cover letter. Never leave the next contact to the hiring manager.

Next, let's drill a little deeper to see what the cover letter must do to get the hiring manager to look at your résumé.

Drilling Deeper into the Cover Letter Strategy

Your cover letter must:

1. **Not be a summary of your education, your duties, or responsibilities that are present on your résumé**. Space on a cover letter is valuable real estate, so don't provide a synopsis of your résumé. The cover letter is more of a sales letter that positions the future benefits of your expertise. Most cover letters rehash the features of a candidate's experience with previous employers. The hiring manager wants to know how your expertise will benefit him or her *going forward*.

2. **Speak to the hiring manager's needs, not your own.** Getting hired is never about you; it's *always* about what the hiring manager needs. You address that by writing a cover letter that ties the benefits of your expertise to what the hiring manager needs (the job ad will provide plenty of clues).

3. **Include quantified accomplishments from your résumé that communicate to the hiring manager that you do, in fact, have a proven track record.** In other words, don't just say "proven track record;" **show it**. A common mistake is just saying you'd be a good fit without supplying the evidence to back it up. Hiring managers understand numbers better than words. The number of arrests you made as a government agent may not mean anything to a hiring manager in the private sector, but your success rate — the percentage — certainly will because it aligns more with the language of the hiring manager.

- If your particular profession doesn't allow for quantitative measures, ask this question after every duty and responsibility in your bullet lists: "How did this duty/responsibility contribute the higher goals of the organization?" If you can't assign numerical values to your achievements, at least you can relate to hiring managers that you understand how what you do is connected to the overall organization objectives.

4. **Grab the hiring manager's attention in 5–7 seconds.** You won't do that by beginning with, "Please find enclosed my resume...". There's no need to inform the hiring manager that you have "attached your résumé" because, if the hiring manager is reading your cover letter, there's a pretty good chance he or she knows a résumé accompanies it. You have a 5–7 second window to grab that hiring manager's interest. In short, **get to the point**, unlike these opening lines from cover letters:

   - "Recently, I learned about a possible position with your company. I am very interested in applying for this position. I believe that my background and experience in this industry makes me an excellent candidate for the open position."

   - "I am writing to express my interest in working as a <position A> or <position B> with your organization. I am a highly talented and dedicated professional with over 25 years of progressive experience in <skill A>, <skill B>, and <skill C>. Now, I would like to bring my expertise and knowledge to work for your organization."

   - "I am excited to see the <position title> with <company name>."

- "I am interested in the position of <position name> posted on your website."
- "I am writing to share my interest in applying for the <position name> as posted on your website. <Position name> has been a strong desire of mine, and my customer service experience at <current employer name> would make a great fit for your organization."

OK, that's enough. None of these opening salvos generates any interest from most hiring managers to read further.

You can start with a rhetorical question such as, "Do you think that Company ABC would want a financial risk management professional who has accomplished the following?" And then you follow that with a short bullet list of quantified accomplishments pulled from your résumé.

Leading with a rhetorical question whose only rational response is "yes" is a tactic that has you escorting the hiring manager deeper into your cover letter and the other accomplishments that support your contention that you're the perfect candidate. It's how the Greek philosopher Socrates was able to win philosophical debates. He kept asking questions that required his opponents to agree with his statements. He continued winning one admission after another until his opponents had no choice but to embrace a conclusion they may have strenuously denied earlier. We call that the Socratic Method of Inquiry.

In fact, Dale Carnegie writes that one of the ways to win people to your way of thinking is to "get the other person saying 'yes, yes' immediately."

5. **Allow you to put on your unabashed self-promoter hat, but** *only* **if you have the quantified accomplishments to back it up.** Writing something like, "When you need that proposal writer who has garnered more than $30 million in government grants and awards, you call me: John Doe" is perfectly legit *if*

that $30 million number is on your résumé. But without the evidence to support that assertion, you're just "all hat, no cattle," as they say here in Texas.

6. **Eliminate "squishy" verbiage.** Your cover letter strategy should be aware that a hiring manager doesn't care that you:

- "Love" your professional specialty
- Are "passionate" about your professional specialty
- Are "confident" he or she will find you qualified for the position
- "Believe" your skills are what the position calls for.

Such "squishy" words don't belong in a cover letter and actually turn off many hiring managers from reading further. Hiring managers understand the essence of your message only through your demonstrated accomplishments and expertise — not through overt statements in a cover letter. A candidate's motivation and desire for a particular type of work is most favorably received verbally as when the candidate describes past accomplishments or problems solved. That initiative and self-drive simply can't be conveyed through statements with nothing to back them up.

7. **Must have more instances of "you/your/yours" than "I/me/my/mine."** The cover letter should always be about how you address the hiring manager's concerns with the benefits of your expertise. You do that using the language of benefits: "you/your/yours." It's what students learn in Copywriting 101 classes — promote the benefits that "you, the consumer" will receive by using this product or service. It's no different with a cover letter.

8. **Always take control of the follow-up in your closing paragraph.** Never write about "hoping to hear from you" or

"thank you for your consideration." Don't write: "If you have any questions, please contact me at..." because hiring managers know how to contact you if they have any questions. That information is on your résumé. Tell the hiring manager you'll call in a few days to discuss further how you're that value-added professional for the position, and then follow through with the phone call.

It doesn't matter if you speak to the hiring manager, to voice mail, or an administrative assistant. Taking control of the follow-up gets your name across the hiring manager's desk again. Keeping your name out front throughout the entire hiring process — especially after interviews are finished — is key to improving your chances of getting the job offer.

Here's an example closing paragraph from a cover letter I've used in my career that includes the promise of calling the hiring manager:

> *I have a 25-year track record of continually adding value to the projects for which I was responsible. I can do the same for your company. I will call you in a few days to discuss how I help you be more successful in an increasingly competitive marketplace.*

And then I make the phone call. It doesn't matter whether I speak to the hiring manager, the administrative assistant, or get voice mail; the point is that my name was brought up again (first in the cover letter; second in the résumé) to the hiring manager. I'm building an associative model in the hiring manager's memory nodes.

What if the job ad says, "No phone calls, please"? That's an easy fix. The closing paragraph now reads like this:

> *I have a 25-year track record of continually adding value to the projects for which I was responsible. I can do the same for your company to help you be more successful in an increasingly competitive marketplace.*

That's a much more powerful closing sentence than the usual drivel found on cover letters about "hoping to hear from you at your earliest convenience." Hiring managers already understand your wanting to schedule an interview.

Now let's look at the different information blocks of a cover letter.

Other Cover Letter Information Blocks

Contact Information

- Only your best email address and phone number is necessary; including a physical address is no longer required.

- Include any pertinent professional designation after your name.

- A LinkedIn URL to a professionally written profile is a must today as it is another tool hiring managers use to evaluate candidates.

Supporting Paragraphs

- Don't repeat information from your résumé unless you are mentioning the bolded (and perhaps quantified) accomplishments that also appear in a bullet list on your résumé.

- Couch your overall expertise and achievements in language that sells hiring managers on your understanding of those issues with which they are contending. Remember, it's all about the benefits of your expertise and less so the features of your experience.

- Present yourself as a professional who is knowledgeable and empathetic to the issues confronting the hiring manager. Getting hired is always about what the hiring manager needs going forward; it is never about you or your awesome experience.

- Scour the job posting for key words and reuse them in your cover letter.

Converting Features of Past Experience to Future Benefits of Expertise in a Cover Letter

Here are a few examples from actual cover letters where the features of previous experience were converted into future benefits of expertise. These are also what I call tactical examples for successful impression management.

Example 1:

Before: "Throughout **my** career, **I** have been able to save both capital and man hours with **my** proven ability managing design and simulation optimization."

After: "**Your** organization will benefit from proven expertise managing design and simulation optimization — preserving capital expense and reducing man hours."

Example 2:

Before: "Not only do **I** know how regulators view and approach issues but **I** also understand the challenges that corporations face in remaining competitive while meeting their regulatory and control requirements."

After: "**You** will need an expert who knows how regulators view and approach issues, and who understands the challenges **your** organization faces in remaining competitive while meeting regulatory and control requirements."

Example 3:

> *Before:* "**My** time spent on audit engagement provided **me** with experience for assessing internal controls, analyzing financial statements, and honing **my** professional skepticism."

> *After:* "**Your** forensic accounting team will benefit from an expert in audit engagement, internal control assessment, financial statement analysis, and sharp professional skepticism."

Impression management language in cover letters has a future-forward tone that suggests to the hiring manager that you are *the* candidate who can bring the hiring manager and his or her team from where they are now to where they want to be.

Henry Ford once said, "If there is one secret of success, it lies in the ability to get the other person's point of view and see things from that person's angle as well as from your own." That's the secret of an effective cover letter that captures the hiring manager's interest, improves your odds of continuing in the hiring process, and adds to your arsenal for creating a unique advantage.

EIGHT: ADVANCED RÉSUMÉ THERAPY

The most important document in your portfolio that attests to your expertise is the résumé, yet so many people fail to grasp the purpose behind it. While it is a record your professional work history, résumés are most often written from a perspective that doesn't consider the hiring manager's interests.

As I've mentioned repeatedly, hiring managers want to hire experts, problem solvers, and solutions providers, and they are looking for evidence of that in résumés. Unfortunately, most résumés are filled with bullet list after bullet list of duties and responsibilities, or task completions passed off as accomplishments. While that information does serve a necessary purpose, hiring managers prefer to know how those duties and responsibilities contributed to the higher strategic objectives of the organization, usually evidenced by accomplishments.

In *Confessions of a Hiring Manager Rev. 2.0 (Second Edition)*, I annotated several good and bad résumé examples and went into detail about those elements of a résumé that catch a hiring manager's interest. I will not repeat all of that information here, but I will delve deeper into some of those elements that give your professional dossier the edge you need to help you get closer to being the hiring manager's candidate of choice. When you can demonstrate to hiring managers that you understand the business, the issues, and the challenges by listing achievements/accomplishments, core competencies, and functional expertise on your résumé—you'll add to that unique advantage that leads to being on the hiring manager's short list for a job offer.

Before we jump in, let me state that I'm always cautioning candidates to mention only those things on a résumé that highlight their complete and total brand as a professional. Leave the personal details, the hobbies, the social, political, or religious causes, the kids, etc. to the coffeepot conversations after you've been hired. Some information can and will be detrimental to your career or job aspirations, no matter how socially conscious you think that information may be. The hiring manager may not share that concern with you, so why destroy your chances of being hired before you've been evaluated on your professional credentials and achievements?

Case in point: The Equal Rights Center and Freedom to Work found that job candidates who listed LGBT-related interests, such as gay rights activism, on their résumés were 23 percent less likely to get a callback from potential employers than their non-LGBT counterparts, even when the LGBT applicants had the better skill set.[23]

Use the Correct Résumé Format for Your Purpose

Recently I have come across hybrid résumés and CVs that bear little resemblance to what hiring managers, HR managers, and other people with hiring responsibilities expect to see. Such non-traditional formats usually don't work in your favor, so I would caution you to be sure you understand the accepted résumé format for the particular position for which you are applying.

---

[23] Aram, Isha. "Resumes with LGBT Info Are Less Likely To Land a Job" *Jezebel*, July 5, 2014, http://jezebel.com/resumes-with-lgbt-info-are-less-likely-to-land-a-job-1600576375.

The Reverse Chronological Format: Looking for a Job in the Same Field

The reverse chronological format is used for changing jobs within a particular profession or field. It's what you'd use when you are looking for a similar position within your current company or with another company in the same or similar field. The order of headings I recommend is: *Contact Information, Professional Summary, Employment History, Education, Certifications/Licenses, Publications* (if relevant), and *Honors/Awards* (recognized within an industry or profession). Most reverse chronological résumés are no more than two pages in length.

The Functional Format: Entering/Re-Entering the Workforce or Changing Careers

The functional format is used for people entering the workforce for the first time, re-entering the workforce after being out of it for some time, and for people who want to change careers. The emphasis in the functional format is the skills, knowledge, and expertise that you can transfer to a new field or profession, not so much the duties and responsibilities tied to your previous position or career. The order of headings I recommend is: *Contact Information, Professional Summary, Table of Functional Expertise* (three-column format with as many rows containing key skills/knowledge/expertise that's relevant for the new field), *List of Employers* (no bullet lists—just employer name, address, your job title and a one-line description of duties), *Certifications/Licenses, Publications* (if relevant), *Honors/Awards, Education.* Here, the hiring manager is interested in the practical application of skills, knowledge, and expertise and less so in past employers.

The *Curriculum Vitae (CV)*: Moving into Academia or Health Care

The *curriculum vitae* (CV) is sometimes used interchangeably (and incorrectly) with the term *résumé*. It is a detailed document with a specific order of information and level of detail for positions within the academic and health care (sometimes legal) communities. The CV elaborates on education, publications, teaching experience, research, conference presentations, and honors/awards. A shorter CV version that highlights an individual's current career focus rather than his or her entire career history is sometimes preferred. Very often CV formats are prescribed by the hiring entity.

For the most part, the résumé and CV formats are used for employee positions. What do you do when you're in business for yourself and want to add more clients or obtain contract work? Well, you use marketing materials that highlight your expertise and accomplishments. There's more of a promotional flavor to these documents than there is with the résumé or CV because you are looking for more *business*, not a job.

Understand the Difference Between Task Completion and Accomplishment

Time and again I receive résumés from individuals who confuse task completion with accomplishment. Here are a few examples of task completions I have observed being passed off as accomplishments on résumés:

- Generated reports for management
- Developed training program for new hires
- Ensured activities were in compliance with applicable laws

The task completion is an expectation of your job; an accomplishment is most often above and beyond the expectation of your normal role and responsibilities. For people who load up résumés with one bullet list after another of duties and responsibilities, the only way to really get noticed above other candidates is to convert that task or duty into a strategic contribution that has higher value to your employer or organization. It's a way of thinking beyond the day-to-day trench duties you are involved with; it's assigning purpose to your efforts.

I came across a great example of this shift in thinking in a story from financial guru Dave Ramsey's book, *How to Have More Than Enough*:[24]

> *Once a journalist happened upon a construction site where he noticed a group of bricklayers going about their jobs. As the journalist observed, he became intrigued by the various manners in which the workers performed their duties. For instance, one fellow moved as slowly as possible and looked extremely bored with his work.*
>
> *"What is it that you are doing here?" the journalist asked.*
>
> *The bricklayer glared back at the journalist, looking disgusted that anyone would ask a question with such an obvious answer. "What do you think I'm doing?" he bristled. "I'm laying bricks."*
>
> *The journalist noticed another worker who seemed to be enjoying his job more than the first man. He had more enthusiasm and seemed to work with more skill. When the journalist asked this man what he was doing, the worker squared his shoulders and replied, "I'm building a wall."*

---

[24] Ramsey, Dave. *How to Have More Than Enough*, (New York: Penguin Group, 2000), p. 83.

A third man caught the journalist's attention. This worker was a joy to watch. One could almost imagine a symphony playing in the background as the craftsman fluidly picked up each brick, prepared it with mortar, and swung it into position. With tremendous pride, he smoothed the extraneous mortar around the edges of each brick, careful to make sure that each brick was placed with precision. It looked as though he thought the entire building would stand or fall according to the way he did his work.

When the journalist asked the third man what he was doing, he stood up with pride and smiled broadly, "I am building a magnificent cathedral to the glory of the Lord," he replied.

Same building, same job description, what the men were doing was the same thing, but the men had different "whys" and that changed the way they approached their daily work.

So, no more laying bricks or building a wall; from now on you're going to be building something magnificent.

For the Last Time: No Objective Statements, Please!

I hammered home in *Confessions of a Hiring Manager Rev. 2.0* the importance of not using an objective statement as a lead-in for résumés. For one thing, it is passé and most hiring managers I have communicated with over my career all agree that it is a euphemism for "I need a job at *your* company to improve *my* skills and enhance *my* marketability."

To restate: A hiring decision is a prediction rife with uncertainty as it depends on some expectation of future performance. Consequently, candidate assessment and selection involves substantial *irreducible unpredictability* about future success. A typical objective statement on a résumé in no way helps mitigate that irreducible unpredictability; therefore, it is useless and occupies valuable real estate on a résumé.

Few things will get a hiring manager to quickly move on to the next résumé in the pile than some poorly worded, self-serving objective statement.

Marc Cenedella, founder of The Ladders, recently penned an article entitled, "Three Ways You're Sabotaging Yourself." One of Marc's issues is with résumés that don't convey an idea of the kind of job a candidate is looking for. Marc writes: "Show them, at the very top of your résumé, what job you want, and why you're qualified for it."[25]

In an otherwise excellent article, Marc seems to be suggesting the use of an objective statement. But he ignores the most important hiring-process caveat: *Getting hired is never about you; it's about what the hiring manager needs.* You sell the hiring manager on why he or she needs your expertise in your cover letter, not in an objective statement on a résumé. The hiring manager's need always has the higher priority than the need of the candidate. Keep that relationship in mind as you write your résumé.

Forget what résumé writers or career coaches write about creating an awe-inspiring *objective* section on your résumé. Your objective, as implied in your crafted cover letter, is to sell the hiring manager on how you can *help that hiring manager solve problems.* Don't use any portion of your résumé to talk about *you* and *your* needs.

Still having doubts? Here are just a few recent objective statements that came across my desk:

- For an electrical engineering position: *To obtain a challenging Test Engineering position with a dynamic high technology company.*

---

[25] TheLadders.com

- For a technical writer position: *A senior-level technical communications position in a company that demands quality documentation focused on customer needs.*
- For a criminal investigation management position: *Seeking a challenging position as a Deputy Chief Investigator where I can pursue my goals and be an important asset in the organization.*

Some organizational psychologists, career counselors, academic advisors and others in similar positions want "evidence-based data" and not personal preference when it comes to the question of the utility of the objective statement. However, asking for "evidence" about the use of objective statements is fruitless because there is no direct cause and effect to which we can assign values. No one is going to claim they did or didn't hire someone solely because of an objective statement on a résumé.

My belief that most hiring managers find the objective statement ineffective is based on my interactions and conversations with other hiring managers over a 25-year career in oil and gas exploration, software development, and microprocessor design. My conclusion also comes from, in part, reviewing about one thousand cover letters and résumés.

I'm no Stephen Hawking but I've had my share of higher math (many decades ago). Therefore, I think the closest one can come to an objective measure (empirical formula) for a subjective problem (the hiring decision) is a statistical approximation (evidence-based data = the personal preference of a majority of hiring managers).

Words Can Hurt You

There are just some words you shouldn't use in a cover letter or résumé because they all have one thing in common (see Table 3) — they are the subjective, non-measurable opinion of the candidate. Hiring managers don't gravitate toward these terms, so avoid using them in your documents.

Table 3. Worst Terms to Use on a Résumé and Cover Letter (from CareerBuilder.com)

Best of breed	Go-getter	Think outside the box
Synergy	Go-to person	Thought leadership
Value add	Results-driven	Team player
Bottom line	Hard worker	Strategic thinker
Dynamic	Self-motivated	Detail-oriented
Proactive	Track record	Responsible for

There are, however, words that pique the interest of the hiring manager when read in a cover letter or résumé (see Table 4).

Table 4. Best Terms to Use on a Résumé and Cover Letter (from CareerBuilder.com)

Achieved	Improved	Trained/mentored
Created	Resolved	Volunteered
Influenced	Increased/decreased	Ideas
Negotiated	Launched	Revenue/profits
Under budget	Won	Costs avoided

Why are these better terms? Because they are usually tied to objective, measurable achievements and accomplishments.

The *Federal Résumé Guide* suggests considering the following "winning words" when creating a federal résumé. No doubt OCR software and job bots are programmed to recognize many if not most of these words. Most would also be well received on résumés for private sector jobs.

Table 5. "Winning Words" to Consider When Creating a Federal Résumé

Action Verbs

Administer	Analyze	Coach
Conduct	Consult	Contact
Contract	Counsel	Design
Develop	Devise	Edit
Establish	Evaluate	Expand
Improve	Manage	Monitor
Motivate	Negotiate	Operate
Organize	Present	Produce
Publish	Recommend	Reorganize
Research	Sponsor	Supervise
Support	Test	Train

Specific Nouns

Accounts	Analysis	Budget
Campaigns	Colleagues	Conference
Courses	Criteria	Document
Facilities	Findings	Goals
Guidance	Institutions	Literature
Litigation	Members	Morale
Needs	Performance	Plans
Policies	Procedures	Products
Projects	Prototypes	Publications
Records	Reports	Requirements
Specification	Study	Surveys

Descriptors

Accurate	Adept	Analytical
Annual	Collaborative	Competent
Congressional	Customers	Definitive
Diverse	Federal	Fiscal
Functional	Implementation	International
Leading	Legal	Long-range
Monthly	National	Numerous
Pioneering	Potential	Professional
Profitable	Qualitative	Quantitative

Resourceful	Scientific	Statistical
Strategic	Successful	

Tips for Creating an Achievement-Focused Résumé

When a résumé overflows with duties and responsibilities, it's a snoozer for hiring managers because *every candidate* has duties and responsibilities. Make a hiring manager go on a fishing expedition for information he or she wants on a résumé, and your chances for further consideration are greatly reduced.

Here's a strategy for creating an achievement-focused résumé:

Situation	*What were the circumstances leading up to the accomplishment?*
Task	*What task were you assigned for this situation?*
Action	*What action(s) did you take to fulfill the task assigned?*
Results	*Where were the results of the actions you took to fulfill the assigned task?*
Restated for résumé	*How would you state this accomplishment in one short sentence for your résumé?*

Here's an example that I worked up for an accomplishment from an older version of my résumé:

Situation	Technical publications function considering going from print to digital/online-only documentation.
Task	Create task force to evaluate costs and savings, organizational impact, timetable.

117

Action	Obtain buy-in from all functional groups affected by shift to online.
Results	Reduced company printing costs by $2.3 million in two years
Restated for résumé	Reduced documentation printing/ distribution costs by $2.3 million in two years with minimal impact to participating organizations.

Breaking down your involvement with various company initiatives and projects using this table format helps you extract an accomplishment that contributes to the strategic objectives of the organization — with or without quantitative data.

Keep a Log of Project Success for Future Use

This sounds like obvious advice, but far too many people think of their project accomplishments only when it's time to update their résumé, often years later. By then, important details may have escaped their memory. Keeping a weekly log of project accomplishments and challenges helps keep you on course throughout the journey through minor adjustments, rather than having to make a major "dead reckoning" midcourse correction or as the project comes to a conclusion.

Here are just a few reasons why you should maintain a detailed project log regardless of the size of the project.

- A log of past project accomplishments not only helps you craft an attention-getting résumé, but also serves as a project history and reference guide for when you encounter the same or similar projects later.

- A detailed project log helps capture your thought processes and how you assimilate, formulate, and execute your ideas throughout the project history.

- When you need talking points for an annual review, promotion opportunity, or job interview, you have the details handy.

- A detailed project log shows you the dead ends you may have been down once, helping you avoid them in the future for similar projects.

- A project log helps you frame your participation as a contribution to the higher strategic objectives of the organization rather than as a task completion if you update your résumé further down the road.

- A detailed project log helps you calculate or obtain reliable quantitative data (dollars earned, costs avoided, percentages improved, etc.) that further demonstrates your value as a solutions provider to the organization.

Participating in internal process improvement initiatives can pepper your résumé with notable accomplishments as well.

Assign Quantitative Value to Your Accomplishments

The best way to cement your value to any organization is to assign *quantitative value* to your accomplishments. Nothing gets the attention of a manager quicker when considering who stays and who goes, who gets the bigger raise or promotion, and who gets called in for an interview than assigning dollar value or percent improvements to project accomplishments.

Qualitative value, on the other hand, is subjective in nature because it uses language that is often relative in its interpretation. Someone who "excels at generating successful government contracts over 15 months" may or may not be more valuable than someone who has "successfully generated \$175M in government contracts over 15 months." But if I'm to hire or promote only one of these two individuals, I'm pretty sure I'm going to select the person who has a demonstrated (that is, backed up with numbers) track record of success. Quantitative value solidifies the perception I have of your ability to solve problems and provide solutions.

Where do you find such information? Talk to the people who track project costs, cost savings, revenue generated — the finance department in your company. They can help you determine relevant numbers. The press is another good source of quantitative information, particularly those online columnists, bloggers, and journals that track new developments, run product comparisons or product benchmarks, and report on corporate and industry trends in your particular field. Mining that information could yield some specific data on projects or initiatives with which you were involved.

If you don't already, start defining, collecting, and interpreting metrics for projects you are working on. Be sure those metrics are meaningful to the intended audience.

When I worked as a research geological oceanographer for NOAA, choosing the proper analytical standards and statistics for research was critical to obtaining taxpayer funds for oceanographic research projects. The metrics used in the field and in the labs were great for studying sediment dispersal patterns on the continental shelf or the engineering stability of seafloor muds, and were simply the language used by those involved with the research.

But NOAA was interested in one thing: What kind of bang for their buck were taxpayers getting? Were our results meaningful to the people paying the bills? We had to translate the results of field and lab evaluations into a language taxpayers could understand: dollars, as expressed in risk assessment costs, environmental assessment costs, and contingency costs associated with the economic development of offshore areas. These became our metrics, and they measured our successes, which we could then communicate to the taxpayer in their language.

Tracking metrics to determine quantitative value of projects under your charge will serve to enhance your value to any organization.

Converting Tasks and Duties to Functional Expertise

The one question candidates can ask of each bulleted item on their résumé is: "And this task led to what higher strategic result for the organization?" The answer will most often elevate an ordinary duty or task into an effort that reveals a connection to higher-order objective.

The following actual examples come from individuals in client organizations. For some folks, the question had to be asked in different ways multiple times to extract more information for determining a functional expertise. These too are tactical examples of successful impression management.

Example 1: U.S. Air Force returning veteran (C-130 crew chief) seeking opportunities in private industry (commercial, private airlines)

- *Original bulleted item:* "Performed C-130 aircraft maintenance at locations around the world."

- *Revised bulleted item:* "Led team that maintained state-of-the-art C-130 military transport aircraft/gunships using a variety of technical skills and knowledge to ensure crew safety, operational readiness, and mission success at strategic locations around the world."

The **task**, as expressed here, becomes a functional expertise that embraces the core competencies of project management, personnel management, aeronautical mechanics, electronics, safety systems, and so on.

Example 2: U.S. Army returning veteran (armored vehicle mechanic) seeking opportunities in private industry (heavy duty mechanic)

- *Original bulleted item:* "Responsible for maintaining several Abrams M1A1 armored vehicles."

- *Revised bulleted item:* "Maintained three state-of-the-art Abrams M1A1 armored vehicles valued at **$13 million** with **XXX hours** Mean Time Between Failure (MBTF) for a **92 percent uptime efficiency rating** to support field operations in Iraq."

Whenever **quantitative values** for an accomplishment can be included, your stock value goes up in the hiring manager's mind.

Example 3: Technical documentation manager seeking new position
- *Original bulleted items:*
  - Led technical publishing initiative for creating database publishing process
  - Managed eCommerce business development plans and proposals
  - Led ISO 9000 Level II quality documentation effort
- *Revised bulleted items:*
  - Led a technical publishing initiative for creating a database publishing process that would yield an estimated **$2.6M savings** in publishing costs over **two years**
  - Managed eCommerce business development plans/ proposals that **generated $10M** in new business in **18 months**
  - Led ISO 9000 Level II quality documentation effort that resulted in **ISO 9000 registration** on the **first audit attempt**

Word of Caution: Beware of Résumé Fraud

What do former Yahoo CEO Scott Thompson, former Los Angeles Superior Court Judge Patrick Couwenberg, former Cabot Electronics CIO James DeHoniesto, and former RadioShack CEO David Edmondson have in common? They all had fraudulent information on their résumés that helped them reach their executive positions. Thompson, DeHoniesto, and Edmondson all resigned after being found out; in Couwenberg's case, he was removed from the bench after lengthy public hearings. Other high-level executives caught with fraudulent information on their résumés include former Etsy CEO Rob Kalin, former MIT admissions dean Marilee Jones, former Bausch & Lomb CEO Ronald Zarrella, former Notre Dame head coach George O'Leary, former Homeland Security senior director Laura Callahan, former U.S. Olympic Committee head Sandra Baldwin, former Sunbeam CEO Al Dunlap, and former CEO and president of Lotus Corporation Jeff Papows.

Are these highly publicized cases of résumé fraud the tip of the iceberg, or are they just isolated instances involving high-profile executives?

According to Marquet International Ltd., a firm that vets corporate executives and conducts extensive due diligence investigations of corporate directors and management teams, they see an "astonishing" amount of résumé fraud in the course of their executive vetting and investigations. "Academic résumé fraud has increased between 20 and 30 percent over the past five decades," says Peter Levine, a background investigator.

According to Marquet International CEO Christopher Marquet, "When executive lies go unchecked, an organization can be tremendously damaged and embarrassed by negative press, lost revenue, loss of reputation, and plunging stock prices." One consulting firm in New York City reported that more than half of the high-tech résumés in their database had employment histories that were misrepresented. Executive search firm CTPartners found that 64 percent of candidates overstate their accomplishments, while 71 percent misrepresent the number of years in a particular position with an employer. Most of the time, however, people augment a title or salary figure in the hopes of negotiating a better compensation package.

Such in-depth executive vetting and background checks can be expensive—anywhere from $5,000 to $20,000, according to the Association of Certified Fraud Examiners. However, many times a simple phone call to a candidate's alma mater can confirm a claimed degree, or a call to a former employer can verify a title, responsibilities, or claimed accomplishments. Too often, hiring managers or a board of directors are so impressed with a candidate's résumé that they get "schmoozed" and fail to perform the due diligence so necessary today, particularly with candidates claiming education, degrees, and experience from overseas.

My list of common résumé "embellishments" seen over my 25 years' experience is pretty much the same as what's being reported by other companies and research. Here are the ten most common résumé fabrications as well as how hiring managers might address them.

1. **Extending employment dates to cover gaps in employment**. This is easy enough to verify by calling the former employer to verify the dates.

2. **Inflating achievements, professional skills, computer software knowledge, and foreign language proficiency**. This claimed knowledge is sometimes more difficult to assess and verify during the screening portion of the hiring process. Testing is possible during interviews, and using situational and behavioral interviewing techniques can help.

3. **Enhancing job titles and responsibilities**. This too is a common résumé embellishment; again, a phone call to a former employer can validate any claimed job title and duties.

4. **Exaggerating education and bogus degrees**. Another familiar embellishment, seen often with highly publicized cases involving executives. In my experience, I mostly have encountered detailed listings of academic and professional courses as attempts to defect attention away from the fact that a candidate does not meet the education prerequisite as set by an employer. The National Student Clearinghouse (www.studentclearinghouse.org) can help with verifying education credentials.

5. **Unexplained employment gaps and periods of self-employment**. There's nothing wrong with gaps in employment so long as the gap can be explained — for example, taking time off for raising a family or returning to school for an advanced degree. However, "serving 5–10 in San Quentin for grand larceny" should raise a flag. Self-employment isn't a sin — I was self-employed for several years after a layoff, and it was a legitimate period of time working for myself.

6. **Omitting past employment**. I've seen a few instances whereby an employment date was extended at one employer to cover the dates from a subsequent position where the employee was fired for some offense or unwarranted behavior. When employment dates are stretched on purpose, hiring managers might think it's usually done to conceal something.

7. **Bogus or outdated credentials**. In a previous chapter, I touted the value of credentials and professional designations to help in career advancement. A 2001 ADP study revealed that 23 percent of applicants falsified certifications and licenses on

their résumés. All it takes is a phone call to the credentialing organization to verify that the candidate holds the designation and is in good standing without censure or other disciplinary actions. Misrepresenting or falsifying credentials can expose employers to liability.

8. **Phony reasons for leaving a previous position**. A recent study by HireRight reports that 11 percent of applicants misrepresent their reason for leaving a previous job. A phone call to a previous employer will verify any claims about leaving the employ of that entity. If an employee is not eligible for rehire, then prudence dictates passing on the candidate.

9. **Providing fraudulent references**. Some hiring managers have encountered applicants who provided their best friends as references — complete with bogus titles and sometimes phony company names. Rather than call the phone number provided with the reference, HR often used search engines to locate the company's primary phone number and start the reference checking from that end.

10. **Misrepresenting military service**. Verifying military service can be difficult and time-consuming. The National Personnel Records Center (www.archives.gov/st-louis) is the central repository of personnel-related records for both the military and civil services of the United States Government. Given the time required to obtain verification, employment offers should be made contingent upon verification of military service records.

Extreme cases of military service misrepresentation may be subject to criminal prosecution. The **Stolen Valor Act of 2013** (Pub.L. 113–12; H.R. 258) is a United States federal law that was passed by the 113th United States Congress. The law amends the federal criminal code to make it a crime for a person to fraudulently claim having received any of a series of particular military decorations with the intention of obtaining money, property, or other tangible benefit from convincing someone that he or she rightfully did receive that award.

Visit the website of Marquet International to read their impressive "Résumé Liars Club" pages — complete with photos!

A thorough background check for potential hires involves more than searching on Google for any negative information. Due diligence for high-dollar executive-level positions demands reviewing criminal records, regulatory measures, civil lawsuits, bankruptcy filings, and media coverage to avoid a possible costly discovery after the fact that your CEO was once involved with smuggling weapons into a foreign country.

Your résumé, like your cover letter, is yet another document in your portfolio that attests to your expertise and accomplishments. Both documents are always written for the benefit of the hiring manager and his or her hiring needs, not you. An achievement-focused résumé that includes quantitative substantiating information and is free of errors (e.g., gaps, typos, and fraudulent claims) should serve as your invitation for an interview.

NINE: FINE-TUNING YOUR JOB INTERVIEW STRATEGY

"I would rather walk the sidewalk in front of a person's office for two hours before an interview than step into that office without a perfectly clear idea of what I was going to say and what that person—from my knowledge of his or her interests and motives—was likely to answer."
— Wallace Donham, Harvard Business School Dean (1919–1942)

In *Confessions of a Hiring Manager Rev. 2.0,* I go into some detail about controlling the job interview and negotiating a salary without leaving money on the table. Those chapters provide a solid understanding of how to formulate an interview strategy and any subsequent salary discussions from the hiring manager's side of the desk.

In the world of applied and industrial psychology, researchers have for decades claimed that there isn't much in the way of empirical evidence that supports the validity of job interviews for determining which candidate gets hired.[26] Be that as it may, in this chapter I'm going to share with you different aspects of the interview process that will take your planning and implementation to the next level and get you closer to creating that unique advantage. Despite the claims of

---

[26] Ulrich, L. and D. Trumbo. "The selection interview since 1949," *Psychological Bulletin, 63,* 1965. pp. 100–116.

academics, the job interview is the environment where your unique advantage begins to gel.

Proven Question for NOT Getting the Job

The Ladders founder Marc Cenedella has an approach to getting hired that runs counter to my experience and that of many other hiring managers. In a blog post entitled, "Proven Question for Getting the Job", he writes that:

> *Over the past decade, I've tried a lot of different thoughts, tricks, and tips for getting you the job. But the one which I've found has been the most consistently successful for people is to ask their future or prospective bosses: "How do I help you get a gold star on your review next year?"*

With all due respect to Marc (we have exchanged emails on the subject of his post), I think he's in the ballpark with his idea but that question is out in left field from the hiring manager's perspective. And "consistently successful"? I doubt it, unless someone is interviewing to be the boss's lackey (Marc insists you can't argue with the numbers, but I haven't seen them).

I once interviewed an individual whose response to the question: "Where do you want to be in five years?" was this: "I want to help you get *your* boss's job so I can have yours." Ambitious? Maybe. Ambitious, presumptuous suck-up? Definitely. Needless to say, he didn't get a job offer. He's probably in Congress now.

Think about this for a minute: What do hiring managers *really* need: a butt-kissing sycophant or someone who will be the value-add problem solver who can make a difference for team, the project, the business unit — and ultimately, the bottom line?

If someone made that "gold-star" pitch to me in an interview, there's no way they'd get to the next level of consideration for the job.

Such a statement suggests (or reveals) to me that this candidate has a short-term goal mindset, a calculated strategy of personal *quid pro quo* ("I'll help you if you help me") rather than one that supports the goals of the organization. Sorry, there's just no room for sycophants on most hiring managers' short lists.

For anyone who remembers the early 1980s movie *Mad Max 2: The Road Warrior* (starring Mel Gibson), one of the antagonists was a heavily muscled character named "The Humongous." One of his sidekicks always referred to him as "the warrior of the wasteland; the ayatollah of rock-and-rolla." The other leading antagonist was a Mohawk-wearing character named "Wez." The sidekick referred to him as "almighty Wez." This sidekick was appropriately named "The Toadie."

I don't care how great the résumé, cover letter, or interview – most hiring managers would never hire a toady.

The Worst Response to an Inevitable Interview Question

The worst response to the inevitable interview question: "So, tell me something about yourself..." is: "What do you want to know?" With a response like that, you likely have just eliminated yourself from further consideration for the position. You've been given a golden opportunity to describe yourself in a way that will be memorable to the interviewer or hiring manager. Remember: you're trying to establish an associative model in the mind of the hiring manager – you're trying to extend your being *memorable*, which began with the great cover letter and résumé that got you the interview. You want to continue that momentum right up to when a job offer is extended.

Here's an actual response I received from a candidate to the question that created a lingering and positive impression with me: "I'm a cello player and kids' soccer coach, involved with the PTA and who enjoys working on challenging projects always with an eye on the bottom line and the customer's success. I do that by...".

131

In one sentence, I learned that: (1) he was a classical musician who enjoyed the challenge of performing complex music (since I'm a classical musician myself, it created a connection); (2) he was involved in his kids' lives and in his community; and (3) his attitude was that of being a problem solver with the success of others in mind.

Yes, I hired him.

Situational Interview Approaches

Some researchers believe a hiring manager should probe a candidate for cultural fitness before asking specific job-related interview questions. Having conversations first about organizational citizenship, values and vision required for on-the-job success, and counterproductive behaviors suggest that the nonconformist candidate will likely be bypassed in favor of someone who agrees with the organization's value system. Sometimes, it's just not the right job or company for corporate culture renegades. The square peg in the round hole rarely works out well in the long term.

Many hiring managers consider a candidate's corporate culture fit to be a critically important factor in any decision to hire, while others think the person-job connection is the most significant variable. It's likely a combination of both to varying degrees, but one common thread is that past performance in a similar corporate environment or position suggests a higher probability of future success. That's where situational interviews provide some insight into that probability.

There is a solid correlation between unstructured interview techniques and wrong hires, so hiring managers have strong incentive to use the *past behavioral interview*, the *group interview, hands-on simulations,* or *think-aloud protocols* to gauge candidates for job openings. Generally, the past behavioral and group interview approaches focus primarily on your past accomplishments and what you did. In that regard, memorizing every detail of your résumé is a distinct advantage.

However, don't be surprised when the hiring manager shows up in the interview with a hard copy of your LinkedIn profile in addition to your résumé, so be sure you know both your résumé and LinkedIn profile backwards and forwards, and that both present a unified persona.

The think-aloud protocol is often used to determine how a candidate would solve some problem, usually having the candidate verbalize the thinking process as he or she works through to a solution. This method is common in the high-tech industry (though gaining popularity in other industries); a candidate may be asked to verbalize a possible solution to a software code problem or implement some change to a digital circuit for a microprocessor while illustrating the solution on a whiteboard.

The advantage of the think-aloud protocol is that it provides the hiring manager with some indication of how you might solve a problem or approach a resolution, and sheds some light on your expertise (*how* something was done). Depending on the type of problem presented, there may not be a single right answer. The framing of the question or challenge simply may be to learn how you process information to arrive at a solution. Be prepared for that scenario.

Sometimes, a solution requires outside-of-the-box thinking.

Going Outside the Box for a Solution to a Problem

A former employer sent me to an intensive weeklong program ("Managing Through People") for first-line managers who were going to become second-line managers. On the morning of Day 1, the meeting room at this remote resort in the Cascade Mountains of Oregon was full of about 120 people seated six to a table. The people at each table were a team for the entire week. We quickly got down to business with the first assignment, which went something like this:

Your team is in an airplane that has crashed in the desert. You all survive but have no food and only small amounts of water. Your radio is damaged but not destroyed. You have a few hand tools, a lighter, a flashlight, and a magnifying glass. Identify your four greatest problems and the best strategy for your survival. You have 30 minutes and then you will present your findings to the group.

Two of my team members (engineers) were former military fighter jet pilots, so they immediately began working up a plan between themselves without asking for input from the rest of us. I listened to them discuss how to proceed, which basically consisted of trying to repair the radio on the plane with the items on the list. The three ladies on the team were intimidated by these two take-charge guys and just sat quietly at the table as "Maverick" and "Goose" hatched their survival plan for the rest of us.

In the meantime, program facilitators were moving around the room, casually observing the discussion and conversations at each of the 20 or so tables. As time was running out on the exercise, it suddenly dawned on me: "The name of this program is 'Managing Through People' and these two jet jockeys have missed the whole point of the exercise!"

The exercise was a kind-of *no-win scenario* — the point of it was to show how, in a group of people, often the stronger personalities assume control and rush from the problem directly to a solution without considering input from others who may have insight into problem analysis or the second correct answer.

When our table was asked about our survival plan, Maverick assumed the spokesman role and briefly described how he and Goose came up with scenarios for sending out an SOS. When the session facilitator asked, "What did you do about food and water?", Maverick replied, "Well, we ran out of time and didn't get that far."

That's when I saw my opportunity.

I stood up and said, "We came up with a plan for food and water," while pointing to the ladies on my team, who gave me a dumbfounded look, as did Maverick and Goose. I continued:

"First, the exercise didn't specify which desert we had crashed in, so we chose the high desert of the southwest United States, specifically, the Colorado Plateau that has nearby forested areas for cover. Second, the exercise didn't specify what time of year, so we chose the spring, which would have provided for lots of fresh meltwater from the nearby Rocky Mountains. Third, small game should be plentiful for food, but if it isn't then we would eat the *sand, which is there…*"

It took a moment before anyone in the room understood the homonym ("…sandwiches there…") play on words, but as people started to get it, they broke out into laughter and applause. I had changed the rules of the game to beat the no-win scenario like Captain James Kirk did in the *Kobayashi Maru* incident (for you *Star Trek* fans). I received the "Most Creative Solution Award" for my response (but didn't get into Star Fleet Academy).

So the problem scenario wasn't about developing a survival plan, it was about being inclusive with all team members and everyone contributing to problem analysis and possible resolution. It was a people problem.

Reframe Your Perceptions of Confidence to Overcome the Impostor Syndrome

Academy Award winning actress Kate Winslet once confessed to feeling like a fraud before going off to a film shoot; fellow actor Don Cheadle felt that everything he was doing as an actor was a "sham and a fraud." Nobel Laureate Maya Angelou, after having written eleven books, feared she too would be "found out" for her perceived impostor status. Researchers think that as many at 70 percent of people suffer from *impostor syndrome* at some point in their lives. And it's not about not having the talent, skill, or ability to perform; it's about *thinking* you don't have talent, skill, or ability to perform that's the problem.

If you find yourself in a new job or new position at work that stretches your skills, knowledge, and experience *and* you are meeting the challenges with success, but still have your doubts — you may be experiencing the effects of the impostor syndrome. It's a psychological experience common among high achievers (that should make you feel better) that occurs when individuals have difficulty internalizing their accomplishments and achievements, even when such triumphs are recognized by others. Such individuals view their success as good luck, perfect timing, or a combination of both.

The impostor syndrome is being seen increasingly in individuals who have changed careers that offer new or different types of on-the-job challenges. There's even a blog for overcoming the impostor syndrome. It's not an officially recognized condition, so your health insurance won't pay for any therapy — at least not yet.

I experienced the impostor syndrome firsthand during my career change from the oil and gas exploration profession to high tech/software development. Fortunately, my first position in the software development field was with a company that developed mapping software for pipelines, so it did allow me to use some of my geology and minimal programming knowledge. However, the core competencies associated with the career shift from the earth sciences to software development were so disparate, I too believed I would soon be "found out."

Despite the accolades I received for the software documentation I wrote and edited, I thought it was all just a fluke; my fear was that eventually my luck with this masquerade would end. It took several years for me to really rid myself of all traces of the impostor syndrome.

That's the only time I have ever experienced a crack in my usual unshakable self-confidence, and I believe that it was the result of the major career transition I had undergone. The impostor syndrome can be an aftereffect of people who are promoted into management positions, because the thinking sometimes goes, "Wait…I'm OK with contributing as a team member, but now I have to manage the same people who were my peers? They won't take me seriously…"

An engineering friend confided in me after I had been working with him for four years that he's felt like an impostor because he didn't graduate from a big-name engineering school or have the impressive high-tech experience many of his peers had. He imagined that one day, someone from HR would be reviewing his résumé very closely and detect his "low-quality" degree and experience. But he was one of the most highly regarded and intelligent engineers in the office. He was the team's "digital Rain Man." Everybody went to him when they had questions about a variety of microprocessors in development. He has since eliminated this thinking.

Ridding ourselves of the impostor syndrome is about rewriting the rules we use to frame how we perceive our self-assurance. To paraphrase poet Robert Browning, a person's reach should exceed his or her grasp because stretching to close that gap is what builds self-confidence as challenges and aspirations become opportunities. Taking confident ownership of your expertise and accomplishments during job interviews and when you are rewarded with the job helps propel you past any self-perceived limitations.

How Nonverbal Behaviors Influence Interviewers

Significant research studies in psychology have noted that increased eye contact, smiling, high energy level, articulate speech, voice modulation, use of hand gestures and head nods by applicants, and even dressing more formally during job interviews produce favorable outcomes such as a second interview or a job offer. Hiring managers judged such applicants to be more alert, assertive, confident, responsible, and resourceful. Such applicants were also evaluated as most likely to receive a job offer *based primarily (but not exclusively) on the hiring managers' impressions of them.*

The first of many articles I wrote for *Toastmasters Magazine* was entitled, "It's Not What You Say; It's How You Look When You Say It That Counts." The article highlighted communication and body language research by noted psychologist Albert Mehrabian, who concluded that the "total liking" of someone discussing their attitudes or feelings about a subject is the sum of three variables: verbal liking (7%); vocal liking (38%); and facial liking (55%).[27]

The job interview as social interaction sets up expected role behaviors for everyone involved. Most applicants know how to apply the appropriate (and learned) nonverbal body language to demonstrate their social skills and motivation.

However, the best indicators for determining a candidate's motivation include the degree of interview preparation (including being on time), articulate responses to questions, and questions the candidate asks the hiring manager.

Don't underestimate the power of nonverbal body language during job interviews; such communication plays to the intuitive approach many if not most hiring managers take toward making a hiring decision. It is another factor for creating that unique advantage.

How to Work Job Interviews at Job or Career Fairs

One of the great benefits of attending conferences is the opportunity to speak with career coaches, hiring managers, and employer representatives at sponsored job/career fairs. In a way, being able to

---

[27] Mehrabian, A. *Silent Messages: Implicit Communication of Emotions and Attitudes.* (Belmont, CA: Wadsworth Publishing Company, 1981).

interview with employer representatives gathered together in one location is sort of like speed dating: you want to show up prepared, be a great listener, and leave a positive first impression that leaves the employer representative wanting to know more about you — and perhaps even discussing a long-term relationship in the way of a job or career.

Large conferences that also sponsor job/career fairs typically are supported by employers with a connection to the conference profession. For example, the very large Society for Human Resource Management (SHRM) would likely have employer representatives attending the conference who might be interviewing candidates for positions with their respective human resources function, such as:

- Federal employment law compliance experts
- Compensation and benefits administrators
- Training and development specialists
- Employment, recruitment, placement specialists
- HR Information System analysts
- Employee assistance plan managers

Non-conference job/career fairs where a variety of companies, agencies, and nonprofits are looking for all types of candidates often attract thousands of applicants. Regardless of which job/career fair you are interested in attending, here are some suggestions that will help you make the event a success.

- **Plan in advance.** Review the list of employers that will be present and which companies will be of interest to your expertise. Follow up by researching the targeted companies to get a feel for the corporate culture and type of work environment. Make a list of "A" employers and "B" employers to visit or schedule interviews.

- **Memorize your pitch (value proposition).** You are the problem-solver and solutions provider they have been seeking, so sell them on the benefits of your expertise and how it will serve the hiring manager/company's interests going forward. You should know every bulleted item on your résumé and be able to speak at length on each one. Be ready to answer the inevitable question: "So, tell me something about yourself..." Keep any idea of salary and benefits out of the discussion; you aren't at that point in the hiring process yet.

- **Dress for success.** Regardless of the type of position for which you are interviewing, dress like the CEO of "You, Inc." Pressed suits, shiny shoes, and impeccable grooming send a message to recruiters and company representatives before the first words come out of your mouth. Company representatives aren't looking for another employee; they are seeking candidates with long-term and upward-mobility potential. It's human nature for the eyes to exert so much influence over that instant impression.

- **Establish your LinkedIn profile before attending the job/career fair.** Many company representatives will first check your LinkedIn profile prior to your meeting. It's a good idea to connect with the company representative on LinkedIn after the job/career fair.

- **Bring plenty of copies of your résumé with you.** Retrieve your one- or two-page error-free résumé from a professional portfolio or briefcase, not a plain manila folder. Be sure to bring a reverse-chronological version (for changing jobs) and a functional version (for changing careers). Make them perfect so you don't feel you have to apologize for anything when you hand a copy to the company representative. Besides an error-free, professional-looking résumé, bring with you a list of references. Unless you are asked for it, *resist the urge to leave it with the employer representative and any other documents and collateral you may have with you.* Company representatives don't want to be lugging reams of paper on the plane with them when they return to their home cities.

- **Don't be a Ralphie**. In the hit seasonal comedy *A Christmas Story*, young Ralphie brings to class a large fruit basket for his teacher. After the teacher thanks him, he remains at her desk, staring and smiling at her, oblivious to the cue that "the moment" is over and he should take his seat.

Don't be a Ralphie. Recognize social cues that your interview is over (interviews at job/career fairs are often abbreviated due to the number of candidates being interviewed). Don't treat the meeting as an excuse to linger in the booth area or intrude on free moments between interviews with the company representative. Close it out by taking control of the follow-up. Think of the encounter as the first of several meetings or communications with the individual or the company. Ask: "I would very much enjoy continuing our discussion on how I can be that value-add asset to the company...should I call you in a week or so?" They won't deduct points here for you taking control of the next contact.

Candidates must present themselves based on the criteria of the position. Prior to any job interview, the hiring manager or HR evaluates the hard requirements followed by evidence on preferred competencies as provided on the résumé. The cover letter should give some glimpse of the candidate's personality.

At the interview, candidates must know how to "frame" the narrative for their expertise; they must know how to position that expertise appropriately; they must know who they are targeting with that narrative; and finally (and most importantly), they must know how their value proposition addresses the hiring manager/employer's needs. Practice your content and delivery with trusted friends so you can get objective feedback and smooth out the rough edges.

Approach every interview as an opportunity to promote yourself as the problem solver for which the company has been looking. Assume an attitude that you are in business for yourself. When you do, you'll discover that a job interview is a chance to show how you can serve others through the benefits of your expertise going forward.

TEN: THE POST-INTERVIEW STRATEGY

CAUTION

ENTER ONLY IF YOU DON'T HAVE A
PROBLEM TAKING CHARGE OF YOUR
OWN CAREER PATH

SOME UNABASHED SELF-
PROMOTING MAY BE REQUIRED

From the candidate's perspective, the hiring process from start to finish must be thought of as the staged release of information designed to provide more details about your expertise and accomplishments as you advance through the hiring cycle. Very few candidates understand this important approach. Too many perceive the interview as an opportunity to dump all kinds of supportive documentation on the hiring manager and the interview team. You want to pique their interest about your expertise along the way, not inundate them all at once (they won't look at it, and it's often seen as an act of desperation).

The post-interview strategies use elements of your *Professional Skills, Knowledge, and Experience Portfolio* (PSKE Portfolio™), which consists of the documentation that attests to your expertise and the professional brand you have developed over your career. Such documentation includes that shown in Table 6, in the order that information is released to the hiring manager/hiring team throughout the hiring process. Documents above the black shaded cells are provided *prior to* interviews; documents in the black shaded areas are provided *at* the interview; documents below the dark shaded cells are provided *after* interviews are finished. Consultants, however, may have to submit all the documents listed in their column before being invited for an interview or to submit a proposal (depending on the industry or client).

Table 6. Elements of a PSKE Portfolio (listed in a typical order of release over the duration of the hiring process)

Permanent Position	Contractor	Consultant
Cover letter	Cover letter or Introductory letter	Introductory letter
Résumé	Résumé	Capabilities brochure
References	References	Client list
Publications list	Publications list	Publications list
Case history (solving a problem)	Case history (solving a problem)	Case history (solving a problem)
Article reprint (pertinent to job)	Article reprint (pertinent to job)	Article reprint (pertinent to project)
"25 Ways I Add Value to Your Organization" brochure*	"25 Ways I Add Value to Your Organization" brochure*	"25 Ways I Add Value to Your Organization" brochure*
Depending on the profession within a particular industry, samples of work may be required.		

This is the last document staged in the continuous promotion approach.

The Continuous Promotion Approach

The *continuous promotion approach* is the term I use to describe a technique for how candidates improve their odds of getting job offers, how contractors receive more contracts, and how consultants sign more new clients. *It is the technique that takes advantage of the inherent irreducible unpredictability by mitigating its impact in the hiring decision process.*

Research into customer-sales relationships shows that customers are more likely to trust sellers when they demonstrate:

- Frequent interaction
- Consistency
- Ability to deliver results

The results are no different for most hiring managers: The hiring manager (customer) trusts that the candidate (the seller) can understand and solve problems his or her organization faces, based on the candidate's individual experience and demonstrated track record of accomplishments and problem-solving abilities. It just so happens that applying the continuous promotion approach to a job strategy embraces these three trust-enhancing behaviors.

The timeline illustration in Figure 11 shows the steps involved in the continuous promotion approach throughout the hiring process.

Figure 11. Various Steps in the Continuous Promotion Approach

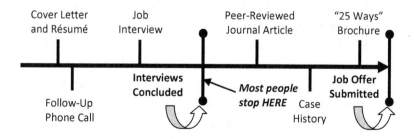

1. Submit attention-getting cover letter/introductory letter, together with:

2. Achievement-oriented résumé or capabilities brochure

3. Follow up with phone call as mentioned in cover letter.

4. Participate in job interview.

5. Several days after all job interviews have concluded, submit (via regular mail) one-page case history write-up of a problem you solved (with Post-It note) to hiring manager.

6. Several days later, submit (via regular mail) copy of peer-reviewed journal article with Post-It note to hiring manager.

7. Several days later, submit "25 Ways I Add Value to Your Organization" brochure with Post-It note to hiring manager.

The continuous promotion approach is about marketing your professional brand throughout the entire hiring process until a hiring decision is made. The vast majority of applicants stop marketing themselves when their interview is over. The continuous promotion approach is an active rather than passive strategy for landing a job, contract, or client.

The most important part of the continuous promotion approach is after the job interviews are finished up until an offer is made. That is when the decision is being made as to who receives the job offer, the contract, or the project. You simply cannot leave it to chance or mercy that you will be selected; you must actively take away the opportunity from the other candidates being considered. You do that through the staged and timed release of documentation in your PSKE Portfolio.

The most effective method for keeping your name at the top of the offer list is to stage the release of these documents as shown in Table 6 throughout the entire hiring process. Typically, the first two items are in possession of the hiring manager before the interview. The remaining documents of the PSKE are staged for release through regular mail, several days apart, after the interview up until an offer is extended or the hiring decision is made.

Whether the hiring manager actually reviews these post-interview testaments (case histories,[28] peer-reviewed journal article,[29] white papers, conference papers,[30] etc.) to your professional brand and expertise is irrelevant; it is the Post-It note you put on each one with your name on it that matters most because it places your name in front of the hiring manager yet again after the interview processes has ended.

I refer to this as the *Trojan horse* technique: it's not about the case history or the article reprint—it's about the accompanying Post-It note that simply says, "Hello <Hiring Manager>…thought you'd be interested in this case history. Signed, <Your Name>." The more often your name and evidence of your brand equity is placed in front of a hiring manager and/or the interview team, the better your chances of getting the job offer, the contract, or the project. It is what's called *the attraction of the familiar*, and that's another facet of your unique advantage.

---

[28] Case history: You've solved an on-the-job problem before, right? Well, write up a one-page case history that: (1) states the problem that had to be solved; (2) assesses the impact to the company; (3) details the solution you provided; and (4) summarizes the benefit to the company.

[29] Peer-reviewed journal article: If you're a professional with seven or more years experience in your technical or professional specialty, and you have NOT had an article published in a peer-reviewed journal read by others in your profession, you are doing your career growth and success a huge disservice. Nothing builds the perception of you as an "expert" more than being published in your field. Hiring managers *want* to hire experts.

[30] White paper, conference paper: Volunteer to provide a presentation for a conference in your field. Typically along with the presentation you'll be asked to provide a paper for the conference proceedings. Again, if you have more than seven years experience in your field, you should already be doing this.

Remember those memory nodes in the associative model mentioned in a previous chapter? They are firing on all cylinders now. The hiring manager's memory nodes are associating you from your previous interactions (cover letter, résumé, and recent interview) with these post-interview documents.

Figure 12 illustrates the Trojan horse technique making use of the Post-It note with a conference paper I had published when I worked in the oil and gas industry. This was the first post-interview document I sent the hiring manager, which was for a position as a project manager for an oil and gas exploration company.

Figure 12. Post-It Note *Trojan Horse* Example.

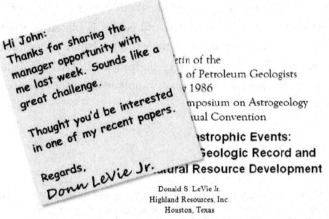

I would follow this document several days later with a case history and similar Post-It note. The last document I would send the hiring manager is the "25 Ways I Add Value to Your Company" brochure, along with the Post-It note that gets right to the point (this example in

Figure 13 is from when I was pursuing a manager position in technical communications, but you can customize this one-page brochure to address the ways you add value for your profession, field, or industry):

Figure 13. *Trojan Horse* Technique with "25 Ways I Add Value" Brochure

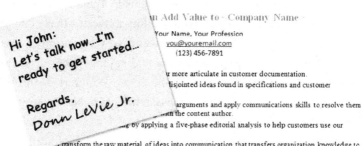

In Add Value to Company Name

Your Name, Your Profession
you@youremail.com
(123) 456-7891

Hi John:
Let's talk now...I'm
ready to get started...

Regards,
Donn Levie Jr.

r more articulate in customer documentation.
lisjointed ideas found in specifications and customer

arguments and apply communications skills to resolve them
with the content author.

by applying a five-phase editorial analysis to help customers use our

transform the raw material of ideas into communication that transfers organization knowledge to customers.

6. I transform the occasional collection of disorganized information into a consistent interface that's presented to customers.

7. I am a technical communications professional skilled in many areas (information architecture, documentation project management, usability engineering, information design, cognitive psychology) and apply those skills to all documentation projects.

8. I make effective use of technical-communication Best Practices to develop better quality user documentation.

9. I have an understanding of the human factors that affect and influence communication.

10. I stay current with practices, tools, technology, and research in my field by being an active member in professional societies.

11. I know and use alternative methods for reaching customer audiences.

12. I help make technical documentation organization invisible to users.

13. When appropriate and so empowered, I remove irrelevant detail from customer documentation so as not to confuse the reader/user with too much information.

Do not discount the psychology behind the hiring process. Often it is the candidate with whom the hiring manager and/or interview team is most familiar who receives the job offer; it is not necessarily the most qualified candidate. Recall that people like what is familiar and similar to them. While other candidates are waiting for word whether they got the job/contract/project, you are establishing yourself with the hiring manager as the only viable option.

The details and much more information about using the continuous promotion approach and the PSKE Portfolio have their own chapters in *Confessions of a Hiring Manager Rev. 2.0 (Second Edition)*, available from bookstores and online book retailers.

The PSKE Portfolio and the continuous promotion approach together use the marketing *Rule of Seven,* which states that up to seven separate contacts may be required before anyone takes action on an offer. You will notice there are seven items in Table 6. The idea of the Rule of Seven is based on the brain's ability to recall — that's one reason your phone number has seven digits and why the number seven is featured in so many popular works and sayings (the seven deadly sins, *The Seven Voyages of Sinbad,* the Seven Wonders of the World, "sailing the Seven Seas," *The Seven Habits of Highly Effective People,* and so on).

Rarely is a hiring decision based solely on qualifications. It is instead the result of multidimensional characteristics possessed by the candidate that address all aspects of succeeding in the workplace — not the least of which are the intangible, subjective variables that often stack the deck in a candidate's favor.

The CPA and Trojan horse technique are tried-and-true methods many others have used to receive a job offer. Does it work every time? No, it doesn't; in fact, it may throw some hiring managers off balance because no one's tried it before. However, over time it works more often than not because over the course of your career you build your brand equity, which increases your attractiveness to hiring managers as the preferred candidate.

ELEVEN: AFTER SAYING "YES" TO THE JOB OFFER

You are ready for your first day on the job; you're excited about the opportunity; the adrenalin is flowing; and your heart is pounding in your chest as you are escorted into your new workspace.

You want to make a favorable impression. You want your new coworkers to know you're fully qualified for the position you've been hired to fill. So you start talking.

And talking.

And immediately you're in the middle of a monologue about your experience or qualifications, or you're jumping into every hallway or cubicle conversation your first week on the job before anyone knows you beyond being "the new person."

Or you may be one of those people who, instead of listening to what is being said *to* them, is already listening to what you are *going to say* when the other person stops talking. That's probably the biggest distraction to listening. You may like to engage in banter with others about your industry or just to get to know people. That's fine, but learn where to cut off such conversations once you've established that positive first impression, because workplace tribal acceptance and credibility takes time to establish.

If you want credibility with coworkers, peers, and managers, do this: Do more listening than talking for at least 30 days. Get a feel for how your fellow team members or coworkers relate to each other by observing with your eyes and ears. Let your output—your *applied*

151

expertise — do the talking for you. The biggest step you can take to gain credibility is to do the job you were hired to do and do it better than expected.

Answer questions when asked and do your best to fit in *gradually* to your work environment. Becoming a new member of a team is a process that occurs in degrees, not all at once, and certainly not on your first day on the job. Don't elaborate on how you would have solved problems differently or how you fixed things at ABC Company. Nobody cares — yet — and if I may politely suggest…

Just shut up, observe, and listen.

You haven't been around long enough to establish any on-the-job credibility ("cubicle cred," as a friend calls it) with your new coworkers, peers, and company. Just getting hired gives you enough authority with others to get by for the first couple of weeks. Talking too much too soon marks you as a know-it-all without having anything to back it up other than your own claims. Remember that only a few people have access to your résumé or have any inkling about your background or accomplishments.

The new coworkers will evaluate you as a member of the tribe based largely on what you accomplish at the new company, how you gel as a team member, and how quickly you understand how things get done. You can do that best by observing *quietly* first before saying too much. Acquire information about the work environment and the corporate political landscape. When in doubt, ask unassuming, nonthreatening questions that serve to clarify or qualify your understanding about how things work.

My friend Steve is president for an association that recently hired a new IT manager. This individual immediately alienated nearly everyone at the association because he had an answer for every kind of problem: Internet technology, HVAC, electrical cabling, personal relationships — you name it. After a recent recommendation (one outside his domain of expertise) that nearly saddled the company with significant unnecessary expense, he was warned about sticking only with what he knows. If only he had shut up and listened for the first few months, he would have maintained the credibility with which he was hired and avoided embarrassment. It may require several internal "reorganizations" or personnel shuffling before the memory of his errors disappears from the corporate environment.

Oliver Wendell Holmes best summed up what speaking and listening convey to others: "It is the province of knowledge to speak and it is the privilege of wisdom to listen."

Don't Be a Cubicle Crawler

Over my career I've seen new employees be a little overzealous trying to fit in as a team member or part of the workplace "neighborhood." Such folks just have to flit from one cubicle to another to have their audience, because what they have to say is *always* more important than any work you may be doing. I also noticed more senior employees who suffer from job or career boredom exhibiting this same behavior. You unknowingly may be a cubicle crawler or have been the victim of one.

Such on-the-job social butterflies rarely consider their sudden presence at your cubicle as an interruption — unless you specifically tell them that it is.

There was a reason why I beat the rush hour traffic to work and got to my desk before nearly everyone else — and it wasn't about being at the office to socialize. I am a morning person, and I needed the quiet of the early morning hours to write, edit, or plan out meetings and to-do lists for myself and my team. I do my best work from early in the morning to about 2pm, and then I hit the doldrums.

Early in my career when cubicle crawlers interrupted my work, I lost time I didn't get back, which sometimes forced me to work through lunch, work late, or take work home. I later learned the only way to prevent such occurrences is to politely nip them in the bud early before they become habits. Once it's a habit with such people, it becomes part of their — and your — routine.

Most people intuitively realize the opportunities for socializing during work hours: getting coffee at the community pot, getting snack or having lunch in the lunchroom, lingering near the networked printer or copier — wherever people naturally gather in common areas. Your cubicle/office should not regularly be one of those places.

Once you allow a cubicle crawler to establish a presence, don't be surprised if it turns into an infestation. Other cubicle crawlers have an uncanny knack for discovering new feeding grounds, and pretty soon you'll have a crowd gathering.

It's not as though these folks don't have work to do; it's just that their daily need for social interaction seems to outweigh your need for getting work done. While such inconsiderate behavior may be oblivious to the offending party, others might notice it for what it is. Your acceptance of these interruptions could be perceived as willful cooperation, so the best approach is to tactfully explain your reasons for coming to work early or for just not being open to interruptions when you are at work in your cubicle or office. If the problem persists, you may have to escalate the issue to management.

If you think you may have cubicle crawler tendencies, please respect the work habits of others; their presence at work is not for your indulgence. If you are being bothered by such behavior, the sooner you initiate the request to stop the interruptions, the quicker the situation becomes a non-issue for everyone involved.

My first experience with a cubicle crawler was a former supervisor of mine when I worked in the oil business. He walked the hallways with a mouthful of chewing tobacco and spit cup in one hand, looking for an opportunity to park himself in someone's office for up to an hour to deliver his off-color monologues. I discovered that the quickest way to have him to leave my office was to ask a geology or geophysics related question, or to spread out my geologic maps on the work table and show him what I'd been working on. Too bad he rarely took his spit cup with him on the way out. Eventually, everyone in the group developed coping mechanisms to keep this supervisor out of their offices.

My last experience was with a hiring consultant who was the first one in the office every morning at 5 a.m.; my mistake was being the second person in the office right after him. You'd think this person would know better or would have caught on through my polite hints that I was busy from the moment I sat down at my desk. But no, he barely gave me time to turn on the computer and check email before he was at my cube: "Whatcha got goin' on today?"

If I simply acknowledged him without turning around at my desk, he would stand there looking out the office window and tell me what the weather was going to do for the next few days. I either had to tell him I was too busy to chat or wait for him to eventually get the message that I was in fact focusing on my work.

He got the nickname "coffee room troll" because as soon as anyone walked in the small coffee room near his cube, he was out of his cube in a flash trying to chat up another victim who only wanted some caffeine to kick-start his or her morning in solitude. He did cause some concern once when he began noting when people arrived at work. He would corner them in the coffee room or hallway and say, "Looks like you got a late start this morning...you didn't get your first cup of coffee until 8:35 when you usually get it at 8:17..." or "Are you keeping banker's hours? You didn't flip on the lights until 6:45 when you usually turn them on at 6:37..." That kind of attention was enough to warrant a conversation with upper management about his behavior. While he was very good at his job, his intrusive personal behavior eventually resulted in his contract not being renewed.

155

Why the Organization May Not Embrace Your Ideas for Change

While many organizations tout their openness to new ideas, innovative process improvement methods, or even quality assurance programs, at a certain level in the organizational fabric, such ideas and programs may never materialize or get implemented for many reasons. There may be budgetary constraints, resource constraints, schedule or time limitations, or—in the grand scheme of the company culture, those ideas or programs don't touch the "heart" of the company business.

Your new company's main business may be designing and manufacturing widgets and getting them into the hands of customers quickly. All other considerations—even a great idea for improving some peripheral process—are secondary to that prime directive. Sometimes an organization's desire to maintain the *status quo*, no matter how broken it may be, just has to be accepted.

However, it you believe your idea has merit despite the potential obstacles for its acceptance, plan your strategy carefully and weigh all the consequences before you offer it to others for consideration. You must be sure that your outcome will be positive. Here are two points to keep in mind:

- Understand the difference between your company's core values and mission/vision statements and the reality of what life is like in the workplace. Such values and statements look good in annual reports for shareholders or in framed posters in the lobby. To be sure, there should be some guiding truths embedded within them, but understand there are unwritten caveats to many core values and mission/vision statements that you won't be aware of until much later in the process.

- If you have ideas for improvements in a process, start locally with your team first. If successful, maybe you and your manager can discuss the positive results with the department or division manager and implement the process improvement at that next level. If that works, let the department/division management take the initiative to push it up higher into the corporate culture. If it is embraced, you'll likely receive some credit; if it is rejected, well, you weren't in the room making the pitch to the higher-ups. All too often in corporate environments, the messenger is linked with the message.

If you are just starting out in your career or in a new job, relax and observe the current company culture, the processes the company uses, and basically how the company does business. Use those first 30 days to just observe how the company culture is manifested in the environment. Company culture is a kaleidoscope of functions that overlap and cooperate to varying degrees, depending on the customer project, the economy, market demands, or whatever the CEO wants to see come to fruition. Discover opportunities for improvement or change by asking questions and listening. Always remember that, as you express your desire to promote an idea or process upward through the organizations, you are navigating in a political environment where sometimes ideas are accepted or rejected based on who is promoting the idea, not on the merits of the idea itself.

TWELVE: MAKING THE JUMP: CAREER TRANSITIONS

From Public Sector to Private Sector

When I left the employ of the federal government in 1980 after three years with the U.S. Department of Commerce–NOAA, I had no problem getting interviews and many job offers from major oil companies who were desperate for experienced geologists.

Today, public sector employees who want to make the transition to the private sector find themselves in a different environment. As we know, government in many respects works quite differently from private businesses. Some individuals find that the cultural shift they need to make to be successful is be a stumbling block. This paradigm change requires time and commitment to grasp how business processes are integrated both vertically and horizontally, and how they all work together to generate revenue and profit ("meeting the numbers").

The good news is that, since 9/11, many federal government agencies have embraced the idea of horizontal integration so they can move further away from rigid "silo" mentalities (i.e., "that's not my department" or "Sorry, I can't help; that's above my pay grade level") and segmented (one after the other rather than simultaneous) responses to changing conditions.

Dynamic exchanges and collaborative processes among many agencies foster cooperation that mitigates risk and threats and can take advantage of opportunities more quickly. Such a shift in how

159

government operates helps minimize past problems of public-to-private-sector transitions.

Let's Get Practical

Let's focus on some practical advice for making the jump to the private sector. First on the agenda: your résumé. Unless you're applying for a fellowship or large grant, or an academic, research, or scientific position at the PhD level—all of which demand a curriculum vitae (CV)—you use a résumé.

I've seen some of the forms the government forces upon workers to document every event of their professional work lives, and that level of detail just won't get the attention of a private sector hiring manager. You have to boil it down to major accomplishments, skills, and experience, and leave the details for another time (such as the interview and the post-interview follow-up).

The Public Sector Résumé

According to the *Federal Résumé Guide*, published by the National Archives and Records Administration,[31] a résumé for public sector positions should include the following information:

- Employer names, addresses, and telephone numbers
- Dates of employment
- Former supervisor's names and phone numbers (at least three professional references, using past current supervisors if possible)
- Your job title/series

---

[31] National Archives and Records Administration, www.archives.gov/careers

- List of your responsibilities
- Salary/GS level and step
- Training
- Career accomplishments
- Awards received
- Education

Current or former federal employees must also submit:

- Last SF-50 (Notification of Personnel Action form)
- Last performance appraisal

The public sector résumé should also include these sections (compare these requirements with those for a private sector résumé):

- *Personal information:* full name; mailing address with ZIP code; area code and phone number; email address; last 4 digits of Social Security number; country of citizenship; and, if applicable, eligibility for veteran's preference
- *Objective statement (optional):* Include what you are seeking, what you can bring to the position.
- *Education:* schools attended, date of degrees awarded, and GPAs
- *Work experience:* job title, employment dates, salary, hours worked per week, employer's name and address, supervisor's name, contact phone number, and whether supervisor can be contacted
- *Other qualifications:* job-related training courses, skills, certificates, honors, awards, professional certifications, special accomplishments, and memberships in professional or honor societies or organizations

This document suggests that candidates use color as a "powerful marketing tool" to create visual appeal or to highlight key information. For résumé length, 1–3 pages is suggested, except for résumés posted in USAJobs (the official job site of the federal government) where the average length is 4–5 pages.

In addition, there may be other documents that must be completed and submitted along with a résumé, such as an online occupational self-assessment questionnaire, transcripts, most recent performance appraisals, or Discharge from Active Duty form.

No wonder candidates are confused about résumé content and format! So much required information to be submitted all at once!

Moving to the Private Sector

You have to understand and be comfortable with the idea that the hiring process in the private sector typically involves the staged release of information over time that provides more detail as you move forward in the process; it's not a document dump at your first opportunity as it is with public sector positions.

First, determine the skills, knowledge, and expertise that you can transfer from the public sector to the private sector. All of that can be dropped into five different buckets:

- Technical abilities/problem solving
- Leadership/relationship building
- Communication clarity
- Ability to influence people and projects
- Business knowledge

Depending on your present position, duties, and responsibilities, some of these categories of transferable skills may already be in good shape.

For individuals exiting the military and seeking jobs in the private sector, communication clarity is typically one area that needs much work. With the possible exception of the high-tech field, most business and interpersonal communication in a business environment does not revolve around obscure acronyms, abbreviations, initialisms, or phraseology ("negatory;" "that's a five by five"). The language style in your cover letter and on your résumé must reflect that of the private-sector hiring manager. Why risk losing his or her interest and attention with arcane terminology? (For more information, see *Confessions of a Hiring Manager Rev. 2.0,* which has an entire chapter devoted to military-to-civilian job market transitions).

To sum up:

- Think résumé, not CV; the hiring process involves the staged release of information *over time.* Extend it past the interview stage by using the continuous promotion approach/Trojan horse technique.

- Categorize your transferable skills using the five buckets (and quantify accomplishments whenever possible to speak to the hiring manager's needs).

- Think transferable skill set → core competency → functional expertise.

- Lose the jargon and unfamiliar terminology in your cover letter and résumé.

Summary of Private-to-Public/Public-to-Private Hiring Process

Public Sector to Private Sector Hiring Process
- Staged release of information throughout process
- Candidate who has more control of what information to provide, how to provide it, and when to provide it

- Hiring decision often influenced by subjective measures
- More focus on how benefits of expertise can help *the bottom line*

Private Sector to Public Sector Hiring Process

- Simultaneous release of information
- Less control of what information to provide, how to provide it, and when to provide it;
- Hiring decision more influenced by objective criteria
- More focus on how experience can support *the mission*

This information on public-to-private-sector transitions could easily be the subject of another book, but is important enough to mention here because the career engagement strategy for the transition is the same as that for people staying within the private sector and simply changing jobs.

THIRTEEN: THEY CAN'T PAY YOU ENOUGH TO BE MISERABLE: TIME TO MOVE ON

Despite all the suggestions, advice, insight, and strategies offered in this book, you may be faced with the prospect of having to leave your current job for greener pastures. You may be working too many hours, performing work above your pay grade or below your level of knowledge and skills, or working for totally inept managers or a boss who's a jerk.

If your misery is temporary, and you recognize that it is, this too shall pass. We all go through periods of hectic project work schedules, and as long as the normal work pace is punctuated *only occasionally* with the frenzied, harried assignment, most of us can tolerate it without too much discomfort. Similarly, incompetent managers are soon found out, so if you can put up with the burr in your saddle for a period of time, you'll still be there after the changing of the guard.

But when the situation is upside-down (where the frenzied, harried schedule is the norm and your company is putting incompetent managers through the jerk-boss rotation), then you must evaluate how long you (and your family) can tolerate such a work environment because it does exact a toll on emotions, health, motivation, and general well-being.

In other words, *they can't pay you enough to be miserable.*

Consider Todd's case: Todd has reached the tipping point in his career as a highly experienced engineering manager for a microprocessor design firm based in California with offices around the world. The owners have created a hugely successful organization. However, as the company has grown, the mom-and-pop management approach has led to longer hours and increased stress that has Todd considering other alternatives in and out of the engineering field.

"Whenever a new project is handed down from executive management, we are told 'you are already two months behind schedule.' So before they even begin, many teams are behind the eight-ball when it comes to project timetables—and how do you close that gap in an industry that accepts extended schedules as the norm?

"In the high-tech engineering world, we have an internal product schedule that is confidential and an external product schedule that is communicated to customers. This external schedule includes some 'padding' to allow for milestone slips, technology challenges, and just not having enough people to do the work. It's a safeguard that helps us deliver products close to what we commit to customers. But I've been in customer meetings where the CEO will announce to the customer that we can deliver our products to them using our internal schedule—all without consulting with the engineering VPs or managers.

"The implications of this CEO's 'saving face' cultural artifact leads to many dozens of employees working 18-hour days, weekends, and even giving up planned and paid-for vacations. I've seen too many capable people being thrown under the bus to save some VP's rear, and I have to wonder when it's going to be my turn.

"I have missed my kids' school and sports activities; I know I'm more stressed than I have been in many years, and, to maintain my sanity and my family relationships, I will have to either move them all into my cube at work, or seek out an alternative career. It's just not worth it."

That's a strong indictment of the high-pressure high-tech work environment, and Todd's situation is not unique. It's the way many companies manage to get products to market, despite the toll it takes on their employees.

Perhaps no one sums up the corporate frustration factor better than *Dilbert®* cartoon creator, Scott Adams. At some point in all of our careers, we've worked for the pointy-haired boss, officed next to coworkers like Wally, and had to endure Catbert-type personalities in human resources. Adams' cartoons in many instances are simply art imitating life — *corporate life*, as he said in the *The Wall Street Journal*:

> *The primary purpose of management is to kill any hope that staying in your current job will work out for you. Bad management is how imagination gets wings. The economy needs workers who are fed up, desperate, and willing to quit their jobs for something better. You can't do something great until first you quit something that isn't. The last thing this world needs is a bunch of dopey-happy workers who can't stop humming and grinning. The economy needs hamster-brained sociopaths in management to drive down the opportunity cost of entrepreneurship. Luckily, we're blessed with an ample supply.[32]*

Want more proof? Here are stories from real people who unknowingly prove Scott Adams' point.

This first story is from former litigation attorney, Sonia Gallagher.

"I am a self-proclaimed retired attorney. I practiced law for six years during which I owned my own practice for the last two years. The stress and lack of work/life balance got to be so much it began to affect my health. I got canker sores, back pains, and migraines on a regular basis. My career was literally affecting my health and my marriage. Deep down, I knew I was lying to myself because I did not enjoy what I was doing. Through introspection exercises, I realized that litigation

---

[32] Adams, Scott. "The Perfect Stimulus: Bad Management," *The Wall Street Journal*, November 6, 2010.

was slowly eating up my soul. I chose to walk away from the law and the money.

"I closed up shop and took a year to create a meditation website, because meditation has had an incredible effect on my life. I wanted to help other high-stress professionals learn how to apply meditation and mindfulness in their daily life. Meditation enabled me to realize my path and calling.

"I am now an executive coach for lawyers and business owners, helping them bridge the gap between the instinctive and the practical to reach higher levels of success in their professional and personal lives. My company's mantra is 'Success through Balance.' I am a walking embodiment of it!"

Freelance writer and former software manager Brenda Murray walked away from a six-figure salary rather than subject herself to the pressure-cooker work environment she found herself in.

"What could be more exciting than contributing to a technology company that was 'Making the World a Better Place' by building software for nonprofit organizations? I left the building in November of 2009. I looked at the large fountain in the marble-floored atrium one last time on my way out and realized it was a mirage. A small thing—a colleague's email—copied to the higher-ups—that my team was incompetent drove me over the edge.

"At my company, these exchanges were encouraged. Coming out on top was more important than doing the right thing. It never occurred to me that constant upper respiratory infections, crying bouts, and my inability to establish a healthy relationship were a side effect of being immersed in a hostile corporate culture. Add in trying to help my brother care for his son who was born with a severe brain injury, and I realized that my six-figure software design manager salary was not worth staying in a value system that didn't reflect my own.

"So I left to become a freelance writer."

Rosemarie Ashley left the mortgage origination field to pursue her true passion: music.

"I was in the mortgage origination industry for 18 years, providing honest and ethical service to Metro-Detroit residents, in a slowly changing market. I was successful despite refraining from deception, fraud, legal violations and unethical practices...until the mid 2000s. Unemployment was high. Families left the state. Property values stagnated then fell.

"By the end of 2007, earning less money than I did when I first began, spending at least 40 hours a week for far less money than I needed to survive. I thought: *If I'm going to work for free, I'm doing what I love.* I closed my branch and pursued my passion full-time. Now, as director of marketing for a small record label, I make music to motivate, inspire, and empower everyday people to meet their true potential."

For these people and many tens of thousands like them, they reached a point where being true to their inner compass and sense of purpose had a higher priority than the rewards they were receiving with their current employers or careers. They took the intrepid leap to discover for themselves what other exciting, fascinating opportunities were awaiting them "out there" — opportunities that didn't involve sacrificing their families, their free time, or their integrity.

FOURTEEN: BECOMING AN AUTHORITY

If you've ever wanted to be that voice of authority that always gets quoted in the business section of the newspaper, is the first person interviewed by TV and radio stations about some important development, or is invited as a frequent keynote speaker at conferences, then perhaps becoming a *pundit*, *sage*, or *guru* — an in-demand authority in your specialty — is your next move.

Dwelling in the land of such giants as Tom Peters, Michael Porter, Don Tapscott, Guy Kawasaki, Richard Branson, Steve Jobs, Tony Robbins, and others requires long-term vision, durable and flexible strategic planning, and an unwavering commitment to continue moving forward to avoid the *one-hit wonder* syndrome.

If the rarified air of that club sounds interesting, then here is a ten-item to-do list to help you get started on staying in demand. There are no secrets here; in fact, this list is simply a recapitulation of much of the information in this book — only at a higher, more focused level — as well as ideas and suggestions from people who are already in demand.

1. Write a book with a hook.
2. Build a platform off your book.
3. Create new buzzwords (dust off your portmanteau).
4. Get busy with promoting and expanding your platform.
5. Be remarkable in a way that makes you memorable.
6. Cultivate friendships with other in-demand authorities.
7. Make your billable authoritative expertise valuable.

8. Balance mental, physical, and spiritual health.

9. Remain modest and keep it real.

10. Don't stop moving forward.

1. **Write a book with a hook.** Nothing says *expert* better than being published. Writing a book is practically a requirement for membership into national or international punditry. You don't have to be a great writer or a former Fortune 500 CEO to qualify as a book author. Just have a message that addresses the current hot topics (visit digg.com; google.com/ trends/hottrends; or trendwatching.com for some ideas) and perhaps a ghostwriter to help you crank out that next *New York Times* bestseller. A literary agent can shepherd your manuscript to a publisher who will offer the best publishing deal.

   If your manuscript includes charts, graphs, tables, and graphics, they can be used in other ways (articles, PowerPoint presentations, blog posts, etc.) your information is packaged and disseminated.

2. **Build a platform off your book.** The master platform builder I learned from is author and consultant Gordon Burgett (gordonburgett.com) who taught me the idea of *topic spoking* my freelance writing nearly twenty years ago. Topic spoking is about finding a core topic that people have an interest in, and then determining all the different formats for presenting that information to different audiences. Your book serves as the information focus from which workshops, seminars, keynote speeches, white papers, articles, blog posts, podcasts, YouTube videos, and perhaps high-dollar consulting opportunities flow.

3. **Create new buzzwords (dust off your portmanteau).** Part of being recognized as sage is the ability to create a new *buzz term*

and tie your branded platform to it. By combining two or more words to create a new one, even old ideas take on new life. The linguistics term used to describe the combination of two or more words and their meanings into a new word that encompasses both meanings is *portmanteau* (a French word, but in England it describes a piece of luggage with two compartments). Here are some portmanteau examples already in use:

- *Smog*: smoke and fog
- *Stagflation*: stagnant economy with inflation
- *Likeonomics*: new global currency consisting of relationships and affinity
- *Momentarianism:* new political term for policies stuck in the present moment
- *Twitterrhea*: no explanation necessary
- *Extremedia:* media outlets that consistently report on events and persons on the periphery of newsworthy mention
- *Orchestrategy:* seasonal marketing plan and performance program for an orchestra
- *Guitarticulation*: sheet music markings for how notes are to be played on a guitar

Fifteen years ago I coined the term *valueocity* to define the speed with which an individual brings value to an organization's higher strategic objectives through efforts above and beyond ordinary duties and responsibilities. I have used valueocity in articles, blog posts, workshops, seminars, and keynote speeches, and it's now the working title of one of my upcoming books: *The Valueocity Quotient: Turbo-Charge Your Career Strategy Inside and Outside the Organization.*

4. Get busy with promoting and expanding your platform.
Don't wait until you've written your book. Articles, blog posts,

PowerPoint presentations, speeches, and even notes on napkins can become seed material for book chapters, seminars, and keynote speeches. You already have some of the material you need to begin your journey to guruhood.

5.   **Be remarkable in a way that makes you memorable.** Strive to be more like Sir Richard Branson and Bill Gates (outrageous stunts aside), whose PR activities are based on substance and backed by a solid team of creative minds. Aim to be less like Kanye West, who has a knack for making himself memorable in unflattering and embarrassing ways. There are ways to garner attention that reflect positively and in a big way on your carefully crafted brand and platform. You do that by showing others a bigger vision of themselves than what they see; you take them to the next level.

6.   **Cultivate friendships with other in-demand authorities.** Nothing accelerates your journey to Yoda-type sagehood better than having well-known personalities cite your work, quote your quips, provide blurbs on the back cover of your books, or invite you to state dinners. There's major influence in circles at that level, so cultivate your "A List" of people who may become your best promoters, spokespersons, and brand/platform expediters. You're only six degrees of separation away from any other person on the planet.

7.   **Make your billable authoritative expertise valuable.** There's no other way of saying it, but when you're making personal appearances, giving a keynote speech, presenting a seminar, or taking on consulting assignments, guru/sage/pundit/Jedi rates apply. It's one of those long-held axioms, but the higher your fees, the more seriously you're taken. Whether it's a keynote address, seminar, or a consulting gig, people hire you

not to confirm what they are doing correctly, but to learn what they are doing wrong and how to fix it. It sounds like an oxymoron, but the better you are at telling people what they don't want to hear, the more they will pay you for it.

8. **Balance mental, physical, and spiritual health.** Yoda was 900 years old when he died; Plato was 81; Peter Drucker was 96. Sageness is bestowed upon those who devote decades of knowledge and experience to solving a plethora of problems. Gurus-in-training understand the importance of nutrition, exercise, spirituality, and other life-enhancing strategies in hastening their ability to attain sage status.

9. **Remain modest and keep it real.** To paraphrase Ralph Waldo Emerson, "A great man is always willing to be little...without being belittling." Although eating crow should be avoided in general, there may be times when it must be part of what Winston Churchill called a "wholesome diet." When it must be consumed, it should be done so in public. A real apology begins with, "I'm sorry *that I*..."; it does not begin with, "I'm sorry *if I*...".

10. **Don't stop moving forward.** You may find yourself wrestling with your ability to tackle one or more of the items on this list. If you believe you can't, then you've set into motion a self-fulfilling prophecy. It's true you can't do them all at once, but you can do some all at once and others in a step-wise fashion over time. None of them involves compromising your ethics or morality, but all of them demand a concerted effort at any level of your career for you to excel at...

   ...the art of the unique advantage.

POSTSCRIPT

When it comes to layoffs and downsizing, I've had my share: eight episodes over my 25-plus-year career in the oil and gas industry and in the high-tech field. Each of those layoffs was as a result of either downturns in the industry or major corporate reorganizations that resulted in the elimination of departments, teams, or positions. Five of those layoffs occurred in the high-tech field — three of which were within two weeks of Christmas, which seems to be a popular time to trim the ranks.

The whole scenario of being let go from your job is uncomfortable. Either your manager or someone from security watches you pack up your personal belongings in a scrounged-up cardboard box as others around you make themselves scarce because they don't know what to say. Or they hover uncomfortably close by like buzzards near road kill, ready to scavenge what you leave behind in your office or cube. Your email access is likely already cut off so you can't send out that last farewell email to your peers and coworkers, and you can't go to the restroom without someone letting you back in the office because you've had to turn in your security access card immediately.

It's the corporate version of the perp walk.

Being laid off — no matter how well prepared you may be emotionally or financially — strikes a blow to your self-esteem because you rarely hear the real reason why you are being let go. However, as you mature in your career, layoffs often become a transition to a better opportunity. You have a wider network of contacts to alert for potential job openings or contracting positions, and, if you've built your personal brand properly, people may already be seeking you out.

Throughout my career, I have always enjoyed building relationships with colleagues; I recognized the importance of having a strong likeability factor whether I was a member of a team, an individual contributor, or a team manager. Eventually, it became one of the features of my personal brand.

A servant attitude is an important part of establishing a likeability factor. Over time, it becomes an expertise for which others will seek you out. You will be seen as a resource, an expediter — someone who can connect people with other people, or people with other ideas. Help others first, but do it without any expectation of reward or favor. Do it because it's the right thing to do and it will pay off huge dividends.

Years ago, the day before my last layoff, I received a LinkedIn request from a friend I had worked with for more than a dozen years. After I got home on the afternoon of my last layoff, I responded to his LinkedIn request and told him that the company had just handed me my walking papers. I let him know that after the first of the year, I'd be looking for some contract work, so if he heard of any opportunities to please let me know.

He responded two minutes later. That weekend he ran into a mutual friend of ours who was asking whether I might be interested in a contract opportunity with his company. The next week, we had lunch; I gave him a copy of my résumé, which was followed up by a phone screen interview with the engineering manager, who hired me on the spot. He told me that I received the highest recommendations from several engineers with whom I had previously worked at other companies, and that I had mastered "the art of the *unfair* advantage." I asked him what he meant by that comment and he replied, "The other qualified candidates just didn't have the brand recognition, list of accomplishments, and professional reputation you have. Every person on the team who had worked with you before highly recommended you."

I have no doubt that the years I spent learning to foster relationships up and down the corporate ladder, helping others succeed in and out of my network, and strengthening the quality of my personal brand were instrumental in getting me back on my feet quickly. I've discovered that once your brand has been established, others will "polish" it (promote it) for you, as my friend did.

Throughout my career, I've observed how friends, coworkers, and others were able to bounce back from layoffs. They did so using many of the strategies and tactics I've detailed in this book and in my seminars. Having said that, will the approaches outlined in this book work for *every* job you apply for and on *every* hiring manager you come across? Absolutely not. What they will do nearly every time is make you and your expertise memorable, which can often lead to your being recommended to other hiring managers, or your being reconsidered for future opportunities. When that happens, you likely can avoid having to "run the gauntlet" of resubmitting cover letters and résumés and go straight to the interview.

While the information presented here is designed to help you get hired or promoted, it's just a part of engaging in strategic career development that also includes:

- **Rethinking** your direction and career goals occasionally
- **Recharging** your attitude with new opportunities (and those periods inbetween opportunities)
- **Revising** your portfolio of supportive documentation to reflect your most current expertise and accomplishments
- **Reloading** your effort with each new challenge
- **Remembering** that your value does not decrease based on someone's inability to see your worth

ABOUT THE AUTHOR

Donn LeVie Jr. has held hiring manager positions at Phillips Petroleum, Motorola SPS, Intel Corporation, and smaller companies while serving in technical and scientific, marketing, and communications capacities.

After receiving his B.S. in geology, Donn worked as a geological oceanographer for the Atlantic Oceanographic and Meteorological Labs (NOAA) in Miami, Florida, for several years before moving to Houston, Texas, where he worked in oil and gas exploration as a geologist for Phillips Petroleum and Highland Resources. He was an adjunct faculty lecturer with the University of Houston Department of Natural Science and Mathematics where he taught undergraduate courses in petroleum exploration and production while working on a Masters degree in geochemistry.

After leaving the oil industry in 1986, he transitioned to the technology sector, which took him into the software engineering and microprocessor design fields where he held various positions in marketing and technical communications.

Over the course of his 30-plus year career, Donn has reviewed more than a thousand résumés and cover letters and interviewed hundreds of candidates for positions in the earth sciences, software engineering, microprocessor design, marketing, and technical communications.

Donn's previous book, *Confessions of a Hiring Manager Rev 2.0 (Second Edition)* was the winner of the 2012 International Book Award for Business/Careers and the Winner of the 2012 Global eBook Award for Careers/Employment.

Today, Donn shares his expertise on strategies for individuals seeking jobs or changing careers, and highlights best practices hiring managers can use for identifying candidates with the highest potential for on-the-job success. Donn also speaks at conferences, college campuses, military installations, trade and business schools, and professional associations where audiences benefit from his extensive expertise and successful career as a hiring manager in various disciplines and industries. He also offers his Career Strategy Services Subscription Program as a discounted member benefit for associations and organizations.

Visit **www.donnleviejrstrategies.com** to find free job and career tip sheets, and articles for every aspect of planning and executing a successful job/career campaign. Dial in to Donn's *Switch ON Your Own Career* blog at his website for regular updates on issues facing job seekers and career changers today. Follow him on Twitter @donnlevie.

APPENDIX A: BRING DONN LeVIE JR. TO YOUR ORGANIZATION

Donn LeVie Jr. works with professional associations, organizations, colleges, business and trade schools, military bases, corporations, and colleges to assist association members and students directly in their job and career endeavors. Donn's approach is one that maximizes efficiencies for organizations and provides a maximum benefit for all involved.

For professional associations and organizations, Donn works through conference organizers at regional, national, and international gatherings by providing cover letter, résumé, and LinkedIn profile evaluations for attendees seeking jobs or career changes. He also works with corporate hiring managers to help them better evaluate candidates for open positions. Donn works with individuals at universities who organize campus-wide career and job fairs.

To be clear, Donn does not offer nor can he offer a guarantee that people will find a job with his personal assistance, as there are other variables beyond any one person's control such as changes in hiring practices, job market fluctuations at different times and in different regions of the country, and the overall up and down of the economy. In fact, he advises you to beware of anyone making *any* kind of guarantee of finding you a job or career, especially if they require an upfront payment. The only guarantee that can be *realistically* offered with services such as a résumé writing service is that you are satisfied that the résumé *someone else wrote* adequately reflects your skills, knowledge, and experience.

Donn's personal assistance will help individuals leverage their skills, knowledge, and experience to their fullest to maximize the chances of getting noticed by hiring managers, getting an interview, and securing an excellent overall compensation package in the shortest time possible. Corporate hiring managers will also benefit from Donn's assistance in fine-tuning hiring strategies for identifying and acquiring the best talent available.

For more information, visit Donn's website at
www.donnleviejrstrategies.com.

What Others Are Saying About Donn LeVie Jr. Seminars, Presentations, and Career Consultations

Here's a sample of what other job seekers and career changers are saying about Donn's personal consultations conducted during national conferences:

"Donn LeVie provided a common-sense approach to solving complex career concerns…he was spot-on with his comments and solutions."

–Chief auditor, Central National Bank

"Donn LeVie gave me practical feedback on my résumé, cover letter, and interview strategy…plenty of takeaways…"

–Chief audit executive, Louisiana Metro Government

"I received valuable career information that can help me NOW...I highly recommend Donn LeVie's focused feedback and tailored assistance..."

–International bank fraud examiner

"I received specific recommendations about my résumé, cover letter, and how to stay in touch with potential employers...I'm glad this wasn't just another 'pep talk' that I hear all too often from other career coaches..."

–Retired accountant

"Donn LeVie provided a solid validation of my current career objective, and his ideas on future opportunities for my expertise were most valuable..."

–Government intelligence analyst

"Donn is an awesome and great resource...His specific recommendations for my résumé and LinkedIn page were most helpful..."

–Auditor, bank executive

"Many thanks, again, for lending your talents to the Career Connection. You definitely added value and we're looking forward to working with you next year!"

–Conference organizer for international anti-fraud organization

From Donn's "Stacking the Deck" seminars:

"You have profoundly affected the way I view work."

"Solid takeaways, which provided tangible guidance for hiring and candidate process."

"Thanks for this session – very beneficial!"

"Great presenter. Great info. Great takeaways. Gave contact info for samples."

"Excellent speaker. A wealth of knowledge and would like to hear him again!"

"It was great! Best speaker of the conference!!"

"So glad I decided to attend this session. Very helpful."

"Lots of good detail! Comprehensive coverage of material. Good info and entertaining stories to emphasize major points."

APPENDIX B: OTHER CAREER STRATEGY BOOKS BY DONN LeVIE, JR.

Confessions of a Hiring Manager Rev. 2.0:
Getting to and Staying at the Top of the Hiring Manager's Short List in a Confused Economy (Kings Crown Publishing)

Available in softcover and all ebook formats $21.00 Retail 280 pages
ISBN 978-1-937678-05-0

WINNER of the 2012 Global eBook Award for Careers/Employment and WINNER of the 2012 International Book Award for Jobs/Careers

The book that set the new standard for career advice! Donn LeVie Jr. has updated his hard-hitting rock-solid advice for job seekers and career changers based on nearly 30 years of reviewing thousands of résumés and cover letters, and interviewing hundreds of candidates for various positions with Fortune 500 companies.

Find out what hiring managers want in a candidate so you can adjust your approach to become the candidate of choice throughout the entire hiring process. *Confessions of a Hiring Manager Rev. 2.0* expands the view from the other side of the desk that reveals the perspectives and expectations hiring managers have of people looking for a job or a new career.

Revised throughout, *Confessions of a Hiring Manager Rev. 2.0* (Second Edition) continues to be the best and only resource for showing people how to create successful jobs and careers from the hiring manager's perspective.

The Valueocity Quotient

Turbo-Charge Your Career Strategy Inside and Outside the Organization (Kings Crown Publishing)
Coming in 2016 (cover concept only)

Valueocity (val-u-ocity: noun) is a blend formed from the words "value" and "velocity" and is a term coined by former Fortune 500 hiring manager, consultant, and award-winning author Donn LeVie Jr. to describe how quickly one delivers quantifiable value to a job, project, or contract and repeatedly providing measurable results that contribute to the higher strategic goals of the organization.

Companies need experts, not employees. Hiring managers are

under increasing pressure by executive management to do a better job finding and hiring candidates who can contribute to the company's overall value proposition. They want people who can demonstrate core competencies and functional expertise that can help build a competitive advantage and market dominance.

In *The Valueocity Quotient*, Donn shows you how to showcase your expertise in such a way that promotes you as the problem solver, solutions provider, and game changer that accelerates your career development for internal and external opportunities, and draws opportunities to you.

It's not enough to have the expertise to add value--smarts and talent aren't enough. Today, you have to be an interesting and influential professional in all your business and professional interactions, regardless of whether you are communicating with a hiring manager or an audience of hundreds or thousands of peers. In effect, when your **valueocity quotient** increases, so does your influence, impact, and income.

More Valuable Career Strategy Resources

The *Confessions of a Hiring Manager* Video Subscription Course

A one-time subscription fee will give you unlimited access to Donn's video course and workbook covering all the details with plenty of examples of cover letters, résumés, interview strategies, how to create an impressive Professional Skills, Knowledge, and Experience (PSKE™) Document Portfolio, and step-by-step instructions on how and when to use those documents to promote your brand and expertise long after interviews have ended. In development for 2016 launch. See Donn's website for details when available.

The *Strategic Career Engagement* Video Subscription Course

This video course with workbook from Donn gets you unlimited access for a one-time subscription fee and delves into creating the strategies and tactics for raising your likeability factor, creating associative models in the minds of hiring managers, defining a solid value proposition for hiring managers, using the language of impression management in cover letters and résumés, enhancing your brand with professional credentials, and becoming an authority in your field. In development for 2016 launch. See Donn's website for details when available.

To receive the latest updates and resources from Donn, visit:

donnleviejrstrategies.com

Donn speaks to all types of professionals on how to create and promote a solid platform for extending a professional brand. He can deliver a keynote address, half-day, or full-day version of the content from any of his books, depending your needs. To obtain details, visit his Services page at:

donnleviejrstrategies.com/services

You can also connect with Donn here:

Blog and Past Presentations: **donnleviejrstrategies.com/blog**
Twitter: **@donnlevie**
LinkedIn: **https://www.linkedin.com/pub/donn-levie-jr/1/300/460**

CPSIA information can be obtained
at www.ICGtesting.com
Printed in the USA
FSOW04n0121211216
28751FS